The Good
Book of Facts

## Bible versions

Versions of the Bible are abbreviated as follows:

AV      Authorized (King James) Version
GNB     Good News Bible
JB      Jerusalem Bible
LB      The Living Bible
NASB    New American Standard Bible
NEB     New English Bible
NIV     New International Version
RAV     Revised Authorized Version (New King James Version)
REB     Revised English Bible
RSV     Revised Standard Version

# The Good News Bible Book of Facts

## Martin H Manser

**Marshall Pickering**
*An Imprint of* HarperCollins*Publishers*

Marshall Pickering is an imprint of
HarperCollins*Religious*
Part of HarperCollins*Publishers*
77–85 Fulham Palace Road, London W6 8JB

First published in Great Britain in 1990 by Marshall Pickering as
*The Amazing Book of Bible Facts*

This edition 1998
Copyright © 1990, 1998 Martin H Manser

Illustrations by Simon Jenkins

Martin H Manser and Simon Jenkins assert the moral right to be identified as the
author and illustrator of this work.

A catalogue record for this book is available from the British Library.

ISBN 0 551 03149 2

Printed and bound in Great Britain by
Caledonian International Book Manufacturing Ltd, Glasgow

# Contents

# Introduction

The Bible is an intriguing book. It is read by millions. It is regarded as one of the world's great books. It remains a world bestseller and has given hope and direction to innumerable people through the ages. It has inspired paintings, poems, musical compositions, plays and films. It is used in law-courts for the taking of oaths. Some have even given their lives for it.

And yet for many of us, the Bible is something of a closed book. We may know parts of the Gospels and some Psalms but fumble hopelessly when asked to find the book of Habakkuk or Philemon. The aim of *The Good News Bible Book of Facts* is to help us all delve more deeply into our Bibles.

In section 1 we look at some basic Bible facts, and give an overview of the books of the Bible and its different translations, to try to see what the Bible is all about.

Many quotations from the Bible have become a firm part of the language, e.g. *escape by the skin of one's teeth, the powers that be,* so section 2 considers the influence of the Bible on English. The stories in section 3 show how for many the Bible provides help and encouragement in life.

So you think you know your Bible? Section 4 has a number of quizzes… what colour was the grass at the feeding of the 5000?; who said 'Can these bones come back to life?'; who was Chuza? The final section gives some practical tips on how reading the Bible can become the adventure of a lifetime. Reading God's word is not only a powerful personal experience; it can also be a constant source of challenge and delight.

*The Good News Bible Book of Facts* has been written to be both an informative and also an inspirational guide. It has been compiled in the hope that readers will discover – or rediscover – a fresh enthusiasm for God's word, the Bible.

Martin H Manser
1998

# Discovering the Bible

## Basic Bible facts

### Chapter and verse

The shortest verse in the Authorized (King James) Version is John 11:35, 'Jesus wept'. In the New International Version Job 3:2 is shorter by letters, 'He said:'. The longest verse is Esther 8:9, a 90-word (AV; 67-word, GNB) description of the edict of the Persian King Ahasuerus (Xerxes) on behalf of the Jews: 'Then were the king's scribes called at that time in the third month, that is, the month Sivan, on the three and twentieth day thereof; and it was written according to all that Mordecai commanded unto the Jews, and to the lieutenants, and the deputies and rulers of the provinces which are from India unto Ethiopia an hundred twenty and seven provinces, unto every province according to the writing thereof, and unto every people after their language, and to the Jews according to their writing, and according to their language.'

In the whole Bible, the middle verse in the Authorized (King James)

Version is Psalm 118:8, 'It is better to trust in the LORD than to put confidence in man.' In the New International Version, the middle verse in the whole Bible is Psalm 106:11: 'The waters covered their adversaries; not one of them survived.'

In the Old Testament the middle verses in the Authorized (King James) Version are 2 Chronicles 20:17–18: 'Ye shall not need to fight in this battle: set yourselves, stand ye still, and see the salvation of the LORD with you, O Judah and Jerusalem: fear not, nor be dismayed; tomorrow go out against them: for the LORD will be with you. And Jehoshaphat bowed

# The Longest Name

The longest personal name in the
Bible is Maher-Shalal-Hash-Baz
(Isaiah 8:1,3) (Good News Bible,
'Quick-Loot-Fast-Plunder'; J.B.
Phillips, 'Quick-pickings-Easyprey').
This was the name given to one of
the sons of Isaiah. The name stood
for the fast defeat of Damascus and
Samaria by the Assyrians: this would
happen before the child would begin
to speak (Isaiah 8:3–4).

his head with his face to the ground:
and all Judah and the inhabitants of
Jerusalem fell before the LORD,
worshipping the LORD.' In the New
International Version the middle verse
in the Old Testament is 2 Chronicles
14:14: 'When they had finished, they
brought the rest of the money to the
king and Jehoiada, and with it were
made articles for the LORD's temple:
articles for the service and for the
burnt offerings, and also dishes and
other objects of gold and silver. As
long as Jehoiada lived, burnt offerings
were presented continually in the
temple of the LORD.'

In the New Testament the middle
verse in the Authorized (King James)
Version is Acts 17:17: 'Therefore
disputed he Paul in the synagogue with
the Jews, and with the devout persons,

and in the market daily with them
that met with him.' In the New
International Version, the middle verse
in the New Testament is Acts 7:9:
'Because the patriarchs were jealous of
Joseph, they sold him as a slave into
Egypt. But God was with him.'

The number of verses in the Bible is as
follows:

## Authorized (King James) Version
Old Testament: 23,214
New Testament: 7,959
Total: 31,173

## Good News Bible
Old Testament: 23,111
New Testament: 7,967
Total: 31,078

## New International Version
Old Testament: 23,145
New Testament: 7,941
Total: 31,086

The longest chapter in the Bible is
Psalm 119 (176 verses); the shortest
Psalm 117 (2 verses). The middle
chapter in the whole Bible is Psalm
117. The middle chapter in the Old
Testament is Job 29. The middle
chapters in the New Testament are
Romans 13 and 14.

The Old Testament contains 39
books (929 chapters); the New

Testament contains 27 books (260 chapters) making a total of 66 books and 1189 chapters.

The two Old Testament books most frequently quoted in the New Testament are Isaiah (419 quotations or allusions) and Psalms (414 quotations or allusions).

The Old Testament verse most frequently quoted in the New Testament is Psalm 110:1, with 18 quotations or allusions.

Chapters in the individual Bible books are shown below:

## Old Testament

| | |
|---|---:|
| Genesis | 50 |
| Exodus | 40 |
| Leviticus | 27 |
| Numbers | 36 |
| Deuteronomy | 34 |
| Joshua | 24 |
| Judges | 21 |
| Ruth | 4 |
| 1 Samuel | 31 |
| 2 Samuel | 24 |
| 1 Kings | 22 |
| 2 Kings | 25 |
| 1 Chronicles | 29 |
| 2 Chronicles | 36 |
| Ezra | 10 |
| Nehemiah | 13 |
| Esther | 10 |
| Job | 42 |
| Psalms | 150 |
| Proverbs | 31 |
| Ecclesiastes | 12 |

## Mini-mini Bibles

The smallest Bible in the world was the tiny *Mite Bible*, published in 1896 by Oxford University Press. Its page size was 1.625 inches by 1.125 inches. The book was 900 pages long and was half an inch thick. It was a typical Victorian curio, produced in large quantities for an eager market at the time.

The smallest New Testament published today, the *Bijou New Testament* (Eyre and Spottiswoode), measures 2.5 by 1.75 inches and has 464 pages.

Song of Songs 8
Isaiah 66
Jeremiah 52
Lamentations 5
Ezekiel 48
Daniel 12
Hosea 14
Joel 3
Amos 9
Obadiah 1
Jonah 4
Micah 7
Nahum 3
Habakkuk 3
Zephaniah 3
Haggai 2
Zechariah 14
Malachi 4

## New Testament

Matthew 28
Mark 16
Luke 24
John 21
Acts 28
Romans 16
1 Corinthians 16
2 Corinthians 13
Galatians 6
Ephesians 6
Philippians 4
Colossians 4
1 Thessalonians 5
2 Thessalonians 3
1 Timothy 6
2 Timothy 4
Titus 3
Philemon 1
Hebrews 13
James 5
1 Peter 3
2 Peter 5
1 John 5
2 John 1
3 John 1
Jude 1
Revelation 22

# An imperfect pangram

A pangram is a meaningful sentence of minimal length that includes all the letters of the alphabet. Ezra 7:21 in the Authorized (King James) Version contains all the letters of the alphabet except 'j': 'And I, even I Artaxerxes the king, do make a decree to all the treasurers which are beyond the river, that whatsoever Ezra the priest, the scribe of the law of the God of heaven, shall require of you, it be done speedily.'

# Words of eternal life

The longest book in the Bible is Psalms (43,743 words in the Authorized (King James) Version); the shortest book is 3 John (294 words).

The average length of a verse is 24.82 words in the Authorized (King James) Version and 23.34 words in both the New International Version and the Good News Bible.

In the whole Bible, the number of words in the Authorized (King James) Version is 773,692; in the New International Version, 752,702; and in the Good News Bible 725,362.

In the Old Testament, the number of words in the Authorized (King James) Version is 592,439; in the Good News Bible 532,665. In the New Testament, the number of words in the Authorized (King James) Version is 181,253; in the Good News Bible, 192,697.

# What is the Bible?

## The Bible: a library of books

The Bible is a collection of 66 books of different kinds of writing: In the Old Testament: the books about God's Law (Genesis through to Deuteronomy), books of history (Joshua through to Esther), books of poetry and wisdom (Job through to Song of Songs), books of the prophets ('the major prophets'. Isaiah through to Daniel; 'the minor prophets', Hosea through to Malachi). In the New Testament: books of biography (the four Gospels of Matthew, Mark, Luke and John), the history of the first Christians (the Acts of the Apostles), letters (Romans through to Jude), and Revelation.

## The Bible's inspired writers

The Bible has a dual authorship. People wrote the books of the Bible, and God wrote it through these people. The immediate authors were people, writers coming from different countries, walks of life, and social positions: kings, e.g. David and Solomon; prophets, e.g. Isaiah and Ezekiel; a tax-collector, Matthew; a doctor, Luke; apostles, e.g. Paul. The ultimate author of the Bible is God: it is his inspired word. See, for example, Mark 7:9–13; Acts 4:25; 28:25; 2 Timothy 3:16.

## The Bible's original languages

There are two main original languages of the Bible: Hebrew and Greek. The Old Testament was written in Hebrew, except for Daniel 2:4–7:28; Ezra 4:8–6:18; 7:12–26; Jeremiah 10:11. These were written in Aramaic. The entire New Testament was written in Greek, the language commonly spoken and written

THE BIBLE IN HIEROGLYPHICS
CONTENTS: GENESIS 1

throughout the Roman Empire in the 1st and 2nd centuries AD.

## The Bible's central message

The Bible has one central message: God's salvation of his people. The Old Testament tells about the origin of human sin and the preparation God made for the solution of this problem through the promise of the Messiah. The New Testament describes the fulfilling of God's plan of salvation in the coming of God's Son, Jesus, the Messiah: his life, death, resurrection and ascension, and the growth of the church, God's redeemed people.

## The Bible's vital importance

Reading the Bible is important because it shows us the way to live. Firstly, and most importantly, *the Bible shows us the way to life*. It shows us that we can have a relationship with Jesus by truly turning away (the Bible word is *repenting*) from our own Godless, anti-God (*sinful*) way of living and turning to God (*believing*).

(See John 1:12; Acts 20:21.) Such believing means personally accepting that Jesus died on the cross to take the punishment due to us for our sin. And as we trust Jesus, and him alone, he saves us and puts us into a right relationship with God. (See Luke 18:9–14; John 3:16; Romans 3:21–28.)

Secondly, *the Bible shows us as Christians the way to live*. Reading the Bible nurtures our faith once we are Christian believers. It is one of God's ways of encouraging Christians to grow stronger, to come to know him better, and to become more like Jesus. Reading the Bible answers such questions as: What is God like? (See, e.g., Psalm 139.) How should we behave at work, at home, in family and society? (See, e.g., Colossians 3:1–4:6.) What is prayer all about? (See, e.g., Luke 11:1–13.) What do I do when the going gets tough in life? (See, e.g., Ephesians 6:10–20 and verses on pages 158f.)

# Bible Overview

## The Old Testament

### THE FIVE BOOKS

The first five books of the Bible tell of the origins of the Jewish race and culture.

**Genesis** The book of beginnings describes creation, the first rebellions against God, and God's choosing of Abraham and his offspring.

**Exodus** God rescued the Israelites from slavery in Egypt and led them to the Sinai Desert. There, he gave Moses the laws to govern the new nation.

**Leviticus** God set up laws for the Israelites, mostly concerning holiness and worship.

**Numbers** Because of their rebellion and disobedience, the Israelites had to wander in a wilderness for 40 years before entering the promised land.

**Deuteronomy** Just before his death, Moses made three emotional farewell speeches, recapping history and warning the Israelites against further mistakes.

### HISTORY BOOKS

The next twelve books continue the history of the Israelites: they moved into the land of Canaan and established a kingdom that lasted almost 500 years.

**Joshua** After Moses' death, Joshua commanded the armies that conquered much of the territory in the promised land.

**Judges** The new nation fell into a series of dismal failures. God raised up leaders called 'judges'.

# The books of the Old Testament

*The great Jehovah speaks to us,*
*In Genesis and Exodus,*
*Leviticus and Numbers see,*
*Followed by Deuteronomy.*
*Joshua and Judges sway the land,*
*Ruth gleans a sheaf with trembling*
*    hand,*
*Samuel and numerous Kings appear,*
*    Whose Chronicles we wondering*
*    hear;*
*Ezra and Nehemiah now,*
*Esther the beauteous mourner show;*
*Job speaks in sighs, David in Psalms,*

*The Proverbs teach to scatter alms.*
*Ecclesiastes then comes on,*
*And the sweet Song of Solomon.*
*Isaiah, Jeremiah then*
*With Lamentations takes his pen.*
*Ezekiel, Daniel, Hosea's lyres*
*Swell Joel, Amos, Obadiah's.*
*Next Jonah, Micah, Nahum come,*
*And lofty Habakkuk finds room,*
*Rapt Zephaniah, Haggai calls,*
*While Zechariah builds the walls;*
*And Malachi, with garments rent,*
*Concludes the ancient Testament.*

**Ruth** This story of love and loyalty between two widows shines out brightly in an otherwise dark period.

**1 Samuel** Samuel became a leader during the transition between the time of the judges and that of the

kings. He appointed Israel's first king, Saul. After his own failure, Saul tried violently to prevent God's king-elect, David, from taking the throne.

**2 Samuel** David, 'a man after God's own heart', brought the nation together. But after committing adultery and murder, he was haunted by family and national crises.

**1 Kings** Solomon succeeded David. In his later years he worshipped the gods of his wives. At his death, a civil war tore the nation apart. The kings who came after him were mostly bad, and the prophet Elijah had dramatic confrontations with King Ahab.

# The Lord's my Shepherd

The hymn, *The Lord's my Shepherd* is based on Psalm 23. The Psalms have inspired numerous other time-honoured hymns and also many modern songs:

Psalm 18:2; 32:7 *Rock of Ages, cleft for me*
Psalm 23 *The King of love my Shepherd is; The Lord's my Shepherd*
Psalm 29:2; 96:9; 116: 13–14 *O worship the Lord in the beauty of holiness*
Psalm 34 *Through all the changing scenes of life*
Psalm 36:5–6; 66:7; 104:1–2 *Immortal, invisible, God only wise*
Psalm 42 *As the deer pants for the water*
Psalm 46 *A safe stronghold our God is still; A mighty fortress is our God (Ein' feste Burg)*
Psalm 46:10 *Be still and know*
Psalm 48:14; 78:14; 105:40 *Guide me, O Thou great Jehovah*
Psalm 61:2 *O safe to the Rock that is higher than I*
Psalm 63:3 *Thy loving kindness is better than life*
Psalm 72 *Hail to the Lord's Anointed; Jesus shall reign where'er the sun*

Psalm 87 *Glorious things of thee are spoken*
Psalm 90 *Our God, our help in ages past*
Psalm 97:1 *The Lord is King; lift up thy voice*
Psalm 98 *Joy to the world! The Lord is come!*
Psalm 100 *All people that on earth do dwell*
Psalm 100:4 *I will enter his gates with thanksgiving in my heart*
Psalm 103 *Praise, my soul the King of heaven; Praise to the Lord, the Almighty, the King of creation*
Psalm 103:1 *Bless the Lord, O my soul*
Psalm 104 *O worship the King*
Psalm 104:33–35 *I will sing unto the Lord as long as I live*
Psalm 105:43–45 *The Lord has led forth*
Psalm 113:3 *From the rising of the sun*
Psalm 118:24 *This is the day that the Lord has made*
Psalm 126:3 *Now thank we all our God*
Psalm 136 *Let us with a gladsome mind*
Psalm 139:23 *Search me, O God, and know my heart today*

# The way of happiness

*Happy are those*
*who reject the advice of evil people,*
*who do not follow the example of*
*    sinners*
*or join those who have no use for*
*    God.*
*Instead, they find joy in obeying*
*the Law of the LORD,*
*and they study it day and night.*
*They are like trees that grow*
*beside a stream,*
*that bear fruit at the right time,*
*and whose leaves do not dry up.*
*They succeed in everything they do.*

*Psalm 1:1–3 (GNB)*

**2 Kings** This book continues the record of the rulers of the divided kingdom. None of the kings of Israel, the northern kingdom, followed God consistently, and so it was finally destroyed by an invader. The southern kingdom, Judah, lasted much longer, but finally Babylon conquered it and deported its citizens.

**1 Chronicles** The book opens with the most complete genealogical record in the Bible, then adds many incidents from the life of David (often the same as those in 2 Samuel).

## 2 Chronicles

Often paralleling the books of Kings, this book records the history of the rulers of Judah, emphasizing the good kings.

**Ezra** After being held captive in Babylon for decades, the Jews were allowed to return to their homeland. Ezra, a priest, went with one of the first waves of refugees, and became a leader.

## Nehemiah

Nehemiah returned from the Babylonian captivity after the temple had been rebuilt. He concentrated on restoring the protective wall around Jerusalem and joined Ezra in leading a religious revival.

**Esther** This story is set among captive Jews in Persia. Esther, a courageous Jewish woman and the queen of the Persian king, foiled a plan to exterminate her people.

## THE BOOKS OF POETRY

Almost one-third of the Old Testament was originally written as poetry. These books concentrate on questions about pain, God, life and love.

**Job** The best man of his day suffered the greatest tragedy. The entire book deals with the question, 'Why?'

**Psalms** These prayers and hymns cover the full range of human emotion; together, they represent a personal journal of how to relate to God. Some were also used in public worship services.

**Proverbs** The proverbs offer advice on every imaginable area of life. The style of wise living described here leads to a fulfilled life.

**Ecclesiastes** A life without God, 'under the sun', leads to meaninglessness and despair, says the Teacher in this strikingly modern book.

**Song of Songs** This beautiful poem celebrates romantic and physical love.

**THE BOOKS OF THE PROPHETS**
During the years when kings ruled Israel and Judah, God spoke through prophets. Though some prophets did predict future events, their primary role was to call God's people back to him.

**Isaiah** The most eloquent of the prophets, Isaiah analysed the failures of all the nations around him and pointed to a future Messiah who would bring peace.

**Jeremiah** Jeremiah led an emotionally tortured life, yet held to his stern message. He spoke to Judah in the last decades before Babylon destroyed the nation.

**Lamentations** All Jeremiah's warnings about Jerusalem came true, and Lamentations records five poems of sorrow for the fallen city.

**Ezekiel** Ezekiel spoke to the Jews who were captive in Babylon. He often used dramatic stories and 'enacted parables' to make his points.

**Daniel** A captive to Babylon, Daniel rose to the office of prime minister. Despite intense political pressure, he lived a model life of integrity and left highly symbolic prophecies about the future.

**Hosea** By marrying a loose-living wife, Hosea lived out his message – that Israel had committed spiritual adultery against God.

**Joel** Beginning with a recent catastrophe in Judah (a locust plague), Joel foretold God's judgment on the nation.

**Amos** A country boy, Amos preached to Israel at the height of its prosperity. His grim warnings focused on materialism.

**Obadiah** Obadiah warned Edom, a nation bordering Judah.

# The books of the Bible

**Jonah** Jonah reluctantly went to Nineveh and found Israel's enemies responsive to God's message.

**Micah** Micah exposed corruption in every level of society, but closed with a promise of forgiveness and restoration.

**Nahum** Long after Judah had stirred Nineveh to repentance, Nahum foretold the mighty city's total destruction.

**Habakkuk** Habakkuk addressed his book to God, not people. In a frank dialogue with God, he discussed problems of suffering and justice.

**Zephaniah** Zephaniah focused on the coming day of the Lord, which would purge Judah. The result of this would be a remnant which would be used to bless the entire world.

**Haggai** After returning from the Babylonian captivity, the Jews began rebuilding the temple of God. But before long they set aside that task to

# The Apocrypha

The Apocrypha consists of a varied collection of Jewish writings from the period between about 300 BC and 100 AD. *Apocrypha*, a Greek word meaning 'hidden things', is used to describe certain books that were included in early Latin and Greek versions of the Scriptures but were excluded from the Hebrew Scriptures.

The Council of Trent (1548) of the Roman Catholic Church accepted the books, apart from 1 and 2 Esdras and the Prayer of Manasses, as part of the Scriptures. According to the Thirty-Nine Articles of the Church of England, the books of the Apocrypha should be read 'for example of life and instruction of manners', but should not be used to establish doctrine. The books of the Apocrypha are:

- 1 Esdras
- 2 Esdras
- Epistle of Jeremy
- Song of the Three Holy Children
- Tobit
- History of Susanna
- Judith
- Bel and the Dragon
- Additions to Esther
- Prayer of Manasses
- Wisdom of Solomon
- 1 Maccabees
- 2 Maccabees
- Ecclesiasticus
- Baruch

work on their own homes. Haggai reminded them to put God first.

**Zechariah** Writing around the same time as Haggai, Zechariah also urged the Jews to work on the temple. He used a more uplifting approach, describing how the temple would point to the coming Messiah.

**Malachi** The last Old Testament prophet, Malachi faced a nation that had grown indifferent. He sought to stir them from apathy.

# The New Testament

### HISTORY BOOKS

The word 'gospel' means 'good news'. Almost half the New Testament consists of four accounts of the life of Jesus and the good news he brought to earth. Each of these four books, or Gospels, has a different focus and a different audience; taken together, they give a complete picture of Jesus' life and teaching. About a third of their pages are devoted to the events of his last week on earth, including the crucifixion and resurrection. Acts continues the story into the period after Jesus left earth.

**Matthew** Written to a Jewish audience, this Gospel links the Old and New Testaments. It presents Jesus as the Messiah and King promised in the Old Testament. Matthew emphasizes Jesus' authority and power.

**Mark**
Mark probably had pragmatic Roman readers in mind. His Gospel stresses action and gives a straightforward, blow-by-blow account of Jesus' work on earth.

**Luke** A doctor, Luke was also a fine writer. His Gospel provides many details of human interest, especially in Jesus' treatment of the poor and needy. A joyful tone characterizes Luke's book.

**John** John's style is more reflective than that of the other Gospel writers.

He selected seven signs that pointed to Jesus as the Son of God and wove together everything else to underscore that point.

**Acts** Acts tells what happened to Jesus' followers after he left them. Peter and Paul soon emerged as leaders of the rapidly spreading church.

### THE LETTERS

The young church was nourished by apostles who set down their beliefs and messages in a series of letters. The first 13 such letters (Romans through to Philemon) were written by the apostle Paul, who led the advance of Christianity to non-Jewish people.

## Paul's letters

**Romans** Written for a sophisticated audience, Romans sets forth theology in a logical, organized form.

**1 Corinthians** A very practical book, 1 Corinthians takes up the problems of a tumultuous church in Corinth: marriage, factions, immorality, public worship and lawsuits.

**2 Corinthians** Paul wrote this follow-up letter to defend himself against a rebellion led by certain false apostles.

**Galatians** A short version of the message of Romans, this book addresses the subject of legalism. It shows how Christ came to bring freedom, not bondage to a set of laws.

**Ephesians** Although written in jail, this letter is Paul's most optimistic and encouraging. It tells of the advantages which a believer has in Christ.

**Philippians** The church at Philippi ranked among Paul's favourites. This friendly letter stresses that joy can be found in any situation.

**Colossians** Written to oppose certain cults, Colossians tells how faith in Christ is complete. Nothing needs to be added to what Christ did.

**1 Thessalonians** Composed early in Paul's ministry, this letter gives a capsule history of one church, as well as Paul's direct advice about specific problems.

# Be what you are!

Warren W. Wiersbe has summed up the message of each New Testament book concisely. Here is a list of the 'Be books' he has written:

| | |
|---|---|
| Matthew | Be Loyal |
| Mark | Be Diligent |
| Luke 1–13 | Be Compassionate |
| Luke 14–24 | Be Courageous |
| John 1–12 | Be Alive |
| John 13–21 | Be Transformed |
| Acts 1–12 | Be Dynamic |
| Acts 13–28 | Be Daring |
| Romans | Be Right |
| 1 Corinthians | Be Wise |
| 2 Corinthians | Be Encouraged |
| Galatians | Be Free |
| Ephesians | Be Rich |
| Philippians | Be Joyful |
| Colossians | Be Complete |
| 1 Thessalonians; 2 Thessalonians | Be Ready |
| 1 & 2 Timothy; Titus | Be Faithful |
| Hebrews | Be Confident |
| James | Be Mature |
| 1 Peter | Be Hopeful |
| 2 Peter; 2 John; 3 John; Jude | Be Alert |
| 1 John | Be Real |
| Revelation | Be Victorious |

**2 Thessalonians** Stronger in tone than his first letter to the Thessalonians, the sequel goes over the same topics, especially the church's questions about Christ's second coming.

**1 Timothy** As Paul neared the end of his life, he chose young men such as Timothy to carry on his work. His two letters to Timothy form a leadership manual for a young pastor.

**2 Timothy** Written just before Paul's death, 2 Timothy contains the apostle's final words to his young assistant.

**Titus** Titus was left in Crete, a notoriously difficult place in which to nurture a church. Paul's letter gave practical advice on how to go about it.

**Philemon** Paul urged Onesimus, the owner of the runaway slave Philemon, to forgive his slave and accept him as a brother in Christ.

## Other letters
**Hebrews** No one knows who wrote Hebrews, but it probably first went to Christians in danger of slipping back into Judaism. It interprets the Old Testament, explaining many Jewish practices as symbols that prepared the way for Christ.

**James** James, a man of action, emphasized the right kind of behaviour for a believer. Someone who calls himself a Christian ought to act like one, James believed, and his letter spells out the specifics.

**1 Peter** Early Christians often met violent opposition, and Peter's letter comforted and encouraged believers who were being persecuted for their faith.

**2 Peter** In contrast to Peter's first letter, this one focused on problems that sprang up from inside the church. It warned against false teachers.

**1 John** John could fill simple words such as *light*, *love* and *life* with deep meaning, and in this letter he elegantly explained basic truths about the Christian life.

**2 John** Warning against false teachers, John counselled churches on how to respond to them.

**3 John** Balancing 2 John, this companion letter mentions the need to be hospitable to true teachers.

**Jude** Jude gives a brief but fiery exposé of heretics.

**Revelation** Abounding with visions and symbols, Revelation is the only New Testament book that concentrates on prophecy. It completes the story, begun in Genesis, of the cosmic battle between good and evil which is being waged on earth. It ends with a picture of a new heaven and a new earth.

# The Bible in English

In the earliest days of English Christianity, the only known Bible was the Latin Vulgate, compiled by Jerome between 383 and 405 AD. This could be read by the clergy and by monks, the only ones who were familiar with the language. In 670 Caedmon, a monk at Whitby, produced in Old English a metrical version of some of the more interesting narratives of the Old Testament.

The first straightforward translation of any part of the Bible into the language of the people was the Psalter, made in about 700 by Aldhelm, the first bishop of Sherborne in Dorset. Some parts of the New Testament were translated into English by Bede, the learned monk of Jarrow, author of the famous *Ecclesiastical History of the English Nation*. According to a letter of his disciple Cuthbert, Bede was still engaged in translating the Gospel of John into English on his deathbed. It is not certain whether he completed it, but, unfortunately, his translation has not survived. King Alfred (871–901) produced during his reign English versions of parts of the Old and New Testaments, including a part of the Psalter. Some Latin gospels that survive from this period have written between the lines what are known as 'glosses', word-for-word translations of the text into English, without regard to the idiom and usage of the vernacular. From the same period as these glosses come what are known as the Wessex Gospels, the first independent Old English version of the gospels. Toward the end of the tenth century Aelfric, Archbishop of Canterbury, translated parts of the first seven books of the Old Testament, as well as part of other Old Testament books.

For nearly three centuries after the Norman Conquest in 1066 the uncertain conditions of the language prevented any real literary progress, but some manuscripts of translations of parts of the Bible into Anglo-Norman French survive. About the beginning of the 13th century an Augustinian monk named Orm or Ormin produced a poetical version of the gospels and the Acts of the Apostles called the *Ormulum*. From the first half of the 14th century there survive two prose translations of the Psalter, in two different dialects; and from the end of the 14th century, a version of the principal New Testament letters – apparently made, however, not for the use of the common people but for monks and nuns. There was no thought as yet of providing ordinary layfolk with the Bible in their own tongue. It was Wycliffe who first entertained this revolutionary idea. And it was he who first made the whole Bible available in English.

# John Wycliffe

Born in Yorkshire about the year 1320, Wycliffe stands out as one of the most illustrious figures of the 14th century. This was a period of transition, neither the Middle Ages nor the Reformation – a kind of middle ground between the two. The

# The book of books

The word 'Bible' is from the Greek *biblia*, which is the plural form of *biblion*. *Biblion* is the diminutive of *biblos*, ('book'), from *byblos* ('papyrus'). In ancient times papyrus was used to make the paper from which books were manufactured. The words *biblion* and *biblia* are used in the Old Testament and the Apocrypha for the Scriptures (Daniel 9:2; 1 Maccabees 1:56; 3:48; 12:9). By about the fifth century AD the Greek Church Fathers applied the term *biblia* to the whole of the Christian Scriptures. Later the word passed into the western church, and although it is really a plural neuter noun, it came to be used in Latin as a feminine singular. Thus 'The Books' became by common consent 'The Book'.

old order was struggling with the new. Throughout the whole of this century the prestige of the Roman Catholic Church was very low. The 'Babylonian Captivity' of the popes at Avignon (1309–1378) was followed by the 'Great Schism', when for forty years there were two rival popes, one at Rome and the other at Avignon. In the struggle between the Papacy and the English Parliament over the papal tribute, Wycliffe sided with Parliament. The outstanding Oxford

# The morning star of the Reformation

John Wycliffe was a student at Balliol College, Oxford, and gradually earned a great reputation as one of the ablest scholars in the University. He was a priest in the Roman Catholic Church, but he rejected transubstantiation, criticized the doctrine of purgatory, and generally expressed great dissatisfaction with the church. This naturally brought him into conflict with the bishops, but he was very popular with the common people, and also enjoyed the protection of John of Gaunt, the king's son.

Wycliffe has been called 'the morning star of the Reformation' and that is undoubtedly a worthy title. In his questioning of the whole structure of the Roman church he was led to do two vitally important things. First, he organized bands of preachers known as the Lollards, who travelled the country preaching the Word of God. This was, by and large, the only instruction the people had in the things of God. Secondly, this remarkable man was responsible for the first Bible in the English language.

(Peter Jeffery, *Christian Handbook*)

theologian of his day and an ardent ecclesiastical reformer, he is called the 'morning star of the Reformation'. He was convinced that the surest way of defeating Rome was to put the Bible into the hands of the common people, and he therefore decided to make such a translation available.

Under his auspices, the Bible came out in 1380–84. It is uncertain exactly how much of the translation was done by Wycliffe himself. A number of scholars worked with him on the project, one of them, Nicholas Hereford, doing the greater part of the Old Testament. The translation was made from the Latin, not from the original languages. Since printing was not then known, copies were made by hand and were naturally very expensive. About 170 are in existence today. The translation was never

> '**Christ and his apostles taught the people in the tongue that was best known to the people. Why should not men do so now?**'
>
> John Wycliffe, Bible translator (1320–84)

printed until 1850, when it was published in four volumes. The original manuscript in the handwriting of at least five different men is preserved in the Bodleian library at Oxford.

To help him in his efforts for reform, Wycliffe organized a kind of religious order of poor preachers, called Lollards, whom he sent throughout England to preach his doctrines and to read the Scriptures to all who wished to hear. Foxe reports that the people were so eager to read it that they would give a whole load of hay for the use of the New Testament for one day. There was opposition to Wycliffe on the part of the church, but contrary to his own expectations, he was permitted to retire to his rectory at Lutterworth, where he quietly died in 1384. Several years later, however, his bones were disinterred and burned, and the ashes scattered over the river that flows through Lutterworth. His translation has indelibly stamped itself on our present-day Bible. Some of the familiar expressions which originated in his version are '*strait gate*', '*make whole*', '*compass land and sea*', '*son of perdition*', '*enter thou into the joy of thy Lord*'.

Four years after Wycliffe's death his secretary, John Purvey, issued a careful revision of his translation, preceded by an interesting prologue and accompanied by notes. The church, however, did not approve of the new Bible. In 1408 a decree known as the *Constitutions of Oxford* was issued, forbidding anyone to translate or read any part of the Bible in the vernacular without the approval of his bishop or of a provincial council. Six years later a law was enacted which stipulated that all people who read the Scriptures in their own language should 'forfeit land, catel, life, and goods from their heyres for ever'. Nicholas Hereford and John Purvey were imprisoned. The public demand for the Bible continued, however, in spite of the severe penalties attached to its circulation.

The 15th and 16th centuries were one of the great epochs of human history. In that time there lived such men as Columbus, Galileo, Francis Bacon and Kepler. Another great man of the time was Gutenberg, the inventor of printing. In 1454 he brought out in Germany the first dated printed work – a Latin Psalter. Two years later he produced the famous Gutenberg Bible, which was a printed version of the Latin Vulgate.

After the capture of Constantinople in 1453, Christian scholars were compelled to leave the capital of the Eastern Empire, where for a thousand years Greek learning had flourished. They brought with them to Western Europe many Greek manuscripts. This led to a revival of interest in biblical studies and made it possible for Erasmus to issue in 1516 the first printed edition of the Greek New Testament. At the beginning of the 16th century Greek was for the first time introduced as a subject of study in the universities of Oxford and Cambridge. By 1500 most of the countries of Europe had the Scriptures in the vernacular. England, however, had only scattered copies of the Wycliffe manuscript version, the language of which had by then become obsolete. The Constitutions of Oxford were still in force. England was ready for a new translation of the Bible, from the original languages.

# William Tyndale

William Tyndale, the next great figure in the history of the English Bible, was born about the year 1494 and

## The nature of God's word

In his introductory note 'unto the Reader' in his New Testament, Tyndale wrote: 'For the nature of God's word is, that whosoever read it or hear it reasoned and disputed before him, it will begin immediately to make him every day better and better, till he be grown into a perfect man in the knowledge of Christ and love of the law of God: or else make him worse and worse, till he be hardened that he openly resist the spirit of God, and then blaspheme, after the example of Pharaoh, Coza, Abiram, Balaam, Judas, Simon Magus and such other.'

spent ten years studying at Oxford and Cambridge. Soon after leaving Cambridge, while working as a chaplain and tutor, he said in a controversy with a clergyman, 'If God spare my life, ere many years I will cause a boy that driveth a plough to know more of the Scripture than thou dost.' This became the fixed resolve of his life. In his projected translation he tried to get the support of the bishop of London, but without success. A wealthy London cloth merchant finally came to his support. However, after six months, in 1524, Tyndale left for the Continent because, he said, he

> ## 'Would this one book were in every language, in every land, before the eyes and in the ears and hearts of all men.'
>
> Martin Luther; when asked to repent of his task of Bible translation

'understood at the last not only that there was no room in my lord of London's palace to translate the New Testament, but also that there was no place to do it in all England, as experience doth now openly declare.' He was never able to return to England. He seems to have visited Luther at Wittenberg. Then he went to Cologne, where he found a printer for his New Testament. A priest discovered his plan, and Tyndale was obliged to flee. In Worms he found another printer, and there, in 1525, three thousand copies of the first printed English New Testament were published. By 1530 six editions, numbering about fifteen thousand copies, had been published. They were all smuggled into England – hidden in bales of cotton, sacks of flour and bundles of flax.

As soon as Tyndale's New Testament reached England, there was a great demand for it: by the laity that they might read it, and by the ecclesiastical authorities that they might destroy it! A decree was issued for its destruction. Bishops bought up whole editions in order to consign them to the flames. As a result, only a few imperfect copies survive. Tyndale's English New Testament began a new epoch in the history of the English Bible. It was not a translation from the Latin, as Wycliffe's had been, but was translated from the original Greek of the text published by Erasmus. With each successive edition, Tyndale made corrections and improvements. So well did Tyndale do his work that the Authorized (King James) Version reproduces about 90 per cent of his New Testament.

After completing the New Testament, Tyndale started to bring out a translation of the Old Testament from the Hebrew text, but he lived only to complete the Pentateuch, Jonah and probably the historical books from Joshua to 2 Chronicles. After ten years on the Continent, mostly in hiding, he was betrayed in Antwerp by an English Roman Catholic and was condemned to death for being a heretic. He was strangled and his body was burned at the stake. His last words were a prayer: 'Lord, open the King of England's eyes.' But Tyndale had won his battle. Although his New Testament was burned in large quantities by the church, it contributed greatly toward creating an appetite for the Bible in English. The government, moreover, began to see the wisdom and necessity of providing the Bible in English for common use. The break with the papacy in 1534 helped greatly in this.

## Miles Coverdale

While Tyndale was imprisoned in Belgium, an English Bible suddenly appeared in England in 1535. It had come from the Continent and was the work of Miles Coverdale, although in the New Testament and in those parts of the Old Testament which had been translated already by Tyndale, it was not more than a slight revision of the latter's work. It was the first complete printed Bible in the English language. It was not translated from the Hebrew and Greek, for in the dedication (to Henry VIII) Coverdale said that he used the work of five different translators, who had written in Latin, German and English. His version of the Psalms still appears in the Book of Common Prayer, the traditional service book of the Church of

'Blessed Lord, who has caused all holy Scriptures to be written for our learning; Grant that we may in such wise hear them, read, mark, learn, and inwardly digest them, that by patience, and comfort of thy holy Word, we may embrace, and ever hold fast the blessed hope of everlasting life, which thou hast given us in our Saviour Jesus Christ. Amen.'
Book of Common Prayer, Collect, second Sunday in Advent.

England. Two new editions of
Coverdale's Bible appeared in 1537,
the title page containing the
significant words, 'Set forth with the
King's most gracious license.' So
within a year of Tyndale's death the
entire Bible was translated, printed
and distributed, apparently with royal
approval.

# Thomas Matthew

In 1537 another Bible appeared in
England, this one by Thomas
Matthew (a pen name for John
Rogers, a former associate of
Tyndale's), who was burned at the
stake by Queen Mary in 1555. The
whole of the New Testament and
about half of the Old Testament
were Tyndale's, while the remainder
was Coverdale's. It too bore on its
title page the words, 'Set forth with
the king's most gracious license.'
This Bible has the distinction of
being the first edition of the whole
English Bible actually to be printed
in England. So now two versions
of the English Bible circulated in
England with the king's permission,
Coverdale's and Matthew's, both
of them heavily dependent on
Tyndale.

# The Great Bible

The next Bible to appear was a
revision of the Matthew Bible, done
by Coverdale. The printing of this
was begun in Paris, but the
Inquisition stepped in and so the
work had to be completed in
England. It appeared in 1539 and was
called the Great Bible because of its
large size and sumptuousness. In his
revision Coverdale made considerable
use of the Hebrew and Greek texts
then available. Subsequent editions
were called Cranmer's Bible because
of a preface he wrote for it in which
he commended the widespread
reading of the Scriptures and declared
that they were the sufficient rule of
faith and life. At the foot of the title
page were the words, 'This is the
Bible appointed to the use of the
churches.' This makes explicit an
order that was issued in 1538, while
this Bible was being printed, that a
copy of it was to be placed in every
church in the land. The people
cordially welcomed the Great Bible,
but its size and cost limited it largely
to use in churches.

The later years of Henry VIII's
reign were marked by a serious
reaction against the reform
movement. In 1543 Parliament
passed an act which banned the use of
Tyndale's New Testament, made it a

# Chapters and verses

The books of the Bible originally had no chapters or verses. For the sake of easy reference, Jews of pre-Talmudic times divided the Old Testament into sections like our chapters and verses. The chapter divisions we use today were made by Stephen Langton, Archbishop of Canterbury, who died in 1228. The division of the New Testament into its present verses is found for the first time in an edition of the Greek New Testament published in 1551 by Robert Stevens, a printer in Paris. In 1555 he also brought out an edition of the Vulgate that was the first version of the entire Bible to appear with our present chapters and verses. The first English Bible to be so divided was the Geneva Bible of 1560.

crime for an unlicensed person to read or expound the Bible publicly to others, and restricted even the private reading of the Bible to the upper classes. Three years later Parliament prohibited the use of all versions except the Great Bible. In London large numbers of copies of Tyndale's New Testament and Coverdale's Bible were burned at St Paul's Cross.

In the brief reign of Edward VI, who succeeded his father Henry VIII in 1547, no new translation work was done. However, great encouragement was given to the reading of the Bible and to the printing of existing versions, and injunctions were reissued that a copy of the Great Bible be placed in every parish church.

# The Geneva Bible

With the accession of Mary in 1553 hundreds of Protestants lost their lives, among them some men closely associated with Bible translation, like John Rogers and Thomas Cranmer. Coverdale escaped martyrdom by fleeing to the Continent. Some of the English Reformers escaped to Geneva, where the leading figure of the Reformation was John Calvin. One of their number, William Whittingham, who had married Calvin's sister, produced in 1557 a revision of the English New Testament. This was the first English New Testament to be printed in roman type and to have the text divided into verses. Whittingham and his associates then undertook the revision of the whole Bible. This appeared in 1560 and is known as the Geneva Bible. It enjoyed a long popularity, going through 160 editions (60 of them during the reign of Queen Elizabeth alone), and continued to be printed even after the publication of the Authorized Version in 1611.

# The Authorized (King James) Version

The Authorized (King James) Version contains many archaic words and meanings, including the following:

| Authorized Version | as in | Revised Authorized translation |
|---|---|---|
| bowels | Philippians 1:8 | affection |
| | Colossians 3:12 | tender mercies |
| conversation | Ephesians 4:22 | conduct |
| | Philippians 3:20 | citizenship |
| leasing | Psalm 4:2; 5:6 | falsehood |
| let | 2 Thessalonians 2:7 | restrain |
| naughty | Jeremiah 24:2 | bad |
| nephews | 1 Timothy 5:4 | grandchildren |
| prevent | Psalm 88:13 | come before |
| privily | Matthew 1:19 | secretly |
| reins | Psalm 7:9 | minds |
| suffer | Mark 10:14 | let |
| verily | Matthew 5:18 | assuredly |
| wist | Luke 2:49 | know |

• Italics are used in the Authorized Version for words which are not found in the original but which are necessary to complete the sense.
• One unexplained feature of the Authorized Version is that the paragraph marks (¶) stop at Acts 20:36.
• The word *and* occurs in the Authorized Version 46,227 times.

# The Bishops' Bible

Queen Elizabeth, who succeeded Mary Tudor as monarch, restored the arrangements of Edward VI. The Great Bible was again placed in every church, and people were encouraged to read the Scriptures. The excellence of the Geneva Bible made obvious the deficiencies of the Great Bible, but some of the Geneva Bible's renderings and marginal notes made it unacceptable to many of the clergy. Archbishop Parker, aided by eight bishops and some other scholars, therefore made a revision of the Great

Bible. This was completed and published in 1568 and came to be known as the Bishops' Bible. It gained considerable circulation, but the Geneva Bible was far more popular and was used more widely.

# The Rheims and Douai Version

This came from the Church of Rome and was the work of Gregory Martin. He and a number of other English Romanists left England at the beginning of Elizabeth's reign and settled in north-east France, where in 1568 they founded a college. The New Testament was published in 1582, while the college was at Rheims – hence it is known as the Rheims New Testament. But the Old Testament was not published until 1609–10, after the college had moved to Douai, and so it is called the Douai Old Testament. The preface warned readers against the then-existing 'profane' translations and blamed Protestants for casting what was holy to dogs. Like Wycliffe's version, this one was made not from the original languages but from Latin, and was therefore only a secondary translation. The main objection to the version was that it adhered too closely to the words of the original Latin and so produced English that was too

latinized. It included the Apocrypha and contained a large number of notes, most of them to interpret the sacred text in conformity with Roman Catholic teaching and to reply to the arguments of the Reformers. The Rheims-Douai Bible in use today is not the same as the one made by Gregory Martin, but is a thorough revision of it made between 1749 and 1763 by Bishop Richard Challoner. It was first authorized for use by American Roman Catholics in 1810.

# Authorized (King James) Version

When Elizabeth died in 1603, the crown passed to James I, who had been king of Scotland for 36 years as James VI. Several months after he ascended the throne of England he called a conference of bishops and Puritan clergy to harmonize the differences that existed in the Church. At this conference Dr John Reynolds, President of Corpus Christi College, Oxford, and a leader of the Puritan party in the Church of England, suggested that a new translation of the Bible be made to replace the Bishops' Bible, which many people found unacceptable. The proposal pleased the king, who violently disliked the Geneva Bible. A resolution was passed to produce a new translation of the

# The American Standard Version

The American scholars who cooperated with the English revisers of the English Revised Version were not entirely satisfied with it. The suggested changes which were printed in an appendix represented only a part of the changes which they wanted to be made. The English revisers retained a large number of words and phrases whose meanings and spellings were regarded as antiquated. Also, they included words which had meanings in America different to those they had in Britain. For these and other reasons the American scholars did not disband when the English Revised Version was published. Their revision of the Revised Version was published in 1901.

The main differences between the English and American revisions are as follows: first, the latter retains the name *Jehovah* in the text, instead of translating it as 'LORD' or 'God'; secondly, it is more strictly uniform in the translation and use of other words. The American Standard Version served as the basis for two other versions, the *Revised Standard Version* and the *New American Standard Bible*.

Bible from the original Hebrew and Greek, without any marginal notes, for the use of all the churches in England.

Without delay King James nominated 54 of the best Hebrew and Greek scholars of the day. Only 47 actually took part in the work, which did not begin until 1607. They were divided into six groups: three for the Old Testament, two for the New Testament, and one for the Apocrypha. Two of the groups met at Oxford, two at Cambridge, and two at Westminster.

Elaborate rules were laid down for their guidance. When a group had completed its task, its work was submitted to twelve men, two from each of the six groups. Final differences of opinion were settled at a general meeting of each group.

In cases of special difficulty, learned men from outside the board of revisers were consulted. Marginal notes were used only to explain Hebrew and Greek words and to draw attention to parallel passages.

The revisers, who received no financial remuneration for their work, completed their task in two years; nine more months were devoted to a revision of their work by a special committee consisting of two members from each group. In 1611 the new version was published. Although the title page described it as 'newly

# Consider the lilies

The Authorized (King James) Version
has been called 'the noblest
monument of English prose'. Read
this version of Matthew 6:28–29:
'And why take ye thought for
raiment? Consider the lilies of the
field, how they grow; they toil not,
neither do they spin. And yet I say
unto you, That even Solomon in all
his glory was not arrayed like one of
these.' Here are ten renderings of
these verses in other versions. Can
you identify the versions? The
answers appear below.

1. And why do you worry about
clothes? See how the lilies of the field
grow. They do not labour or spin. Yet
I tell you that not even Solomon in all
his splendour was dressed like one of
these.

2. And why worry about clothes?
Look how the wild flowers grow: they
do not work or make clothes for
themselves. But I tell you that not
even King Solomon with all his
wealth had clothes as beautiful as
one of these flowers.

3. And why are you anxious about
clothing? Observe how the lilies of
the field grow; they do not toil nor do
they spin, yet I say to you that even
Solomon in all his glory did not clothe
himself like one of these.

4. And why worry about clothing?
Think of the flowers growing in the
fields; they never have to work or
spin; yet I assure you that not even
Solomon in all his royal robes was
clothed like one of these.

5. And why worry about your
clothes? Look at the field lilies! They
don't worry about theirs. Yet King
Solomon in all his glory was not
clothed as beautifully as they.

6. So why do you worry about
clothing? Consider the lilies of the
field, how they grow; they neither toil
nor spin; and yet I say to you that
even Solomon in all his glory was not
arrayed like one of these.

7. And why do you worry about
clothes? Consider how the wild
flowers grow. They neither work nor
weave, but I tell you that even
Solomon in all his glory was not
arrayed like one of these!

8. And why are you anxious about
clothing? Consider the lilies of the
field, how they grow; they neither toil
nor spin; yet I tell you, even Solomon
in all his glory was not arrayed like
one of these.

9. And why be anxious about
clothes? Consider how the lilies grow
in the fields; they do not work, they
do not spin; yet I tell you, even
Solomon in all his splendour was not
attired like one of them.

10. And why should you be anxious
about clothes? Consider the lilies of
the field and learn thoroughly how
they grow; they neither toil nor spin;
Yet I tell you, even Solomon in all his
magnificence (excellence, dignity and
grace) was not arrayed like one of
these.

# American and British English

George Bernard Shaw noted that Britain and America are 'one people divided by a common language'. Here are some examples of major word differences between the US and the UK editions of the New International Version.

| Reference | US edition | UK edition |
|---|---|---|
| Genesis 15:17 | firepot | brazier |
| Genesis 23:17 | deeded | legally made over |
| Genesis 41:5 | heads of grain | ears of corn |
| Genesis 45:1 | have everyone | make everyone |
| Genesis 49:24 | limber | supple |
| Exodus 9:31 | had headed | was in the ear |
| Exodus 33:11 | aide | assistant |
| Numbers 30:2 | obligate | bind |
| Numbers 31:51 | crafted | handcrafted |
| Numbers 35:20 | shoves | pushes |
| Joshua 4:18 | at flood stage | in flood |
| 1 Samuel 13:4 | a stench | an offence |
| 1 Samuel 28:24 | butchered | slaughtered |
| 2 Chronicles 2:9 | lumber | timber |
| Esther 2:11 | back and forth | to and fro |
| Proverbs 30:31 | rooster | cock |
| Mark 14:68 | entryway | entrance |
| Acts 9:21 | raised havoc | caused havoc |
| Acts 17:9 | made … post bond | put…on bail |

translated out of the original tongues' and as 'appointed to be read in churches' neither statement is entirely in accord with the facts. The work was actually a revision of the Bishops' Bible on the basis of the Hebrew and Greek; and it was never officially sanctioned by the king, Parliament, or the church. It did not win immediate universal acceptance, taking almost 50 years to displace the Geneva Bible in popular favour.

In the course of time slight alterations were made, especially in spelling, in order to make the Authorized (King James) Version conform to changing usage, but these were all done piecemeal by private enterprise.

# English Revised Version

This version was seen as necessary for a number of reasons: (1) since its publication some words in the Authorized (King James) Version had become obsolete, (2) a number of Greek manuscripts had been discovered which predated those available to the Authorized Version translators, and (3) scholars' knowledge of the Hebrew language had improved.

At the Church of England's Convocation of Canterbury in 1870 a committee was appointed to invite outstanding Hebrew and Greek scholars, irrespective of religious denomination, to join in revising the Authorized Version. Eventually a committee of 54 was formed, divided into two groups of 27 each – one for the Old Testament, the other for the New Testament. American scholars were also invited to cooperate, and they formed two groups corresponding to the British ones. It was agreed that American suggestions not accepted by the British revisers would be recorded in an appendix to the published volume, and that the American revisers would give their moral support to the new Bible and not issue an edition of their own until at least 14 years later. The revisers were guided by a number of rules, the most important being that they were to make as few alterations as possible to the text of the Authorized Version, while basing their translation on a different Greek text.

Altogether the Greek text underlying the revised New Testament differed in 5,788 cases from that used by the Authorized (King James) Version translators. Only about a quarter of these made any material different to the substance of the text, and none so seriously as to affect major Christian doctrines. In the English text of the New Testament there were about 36,000 changes. The new Bible differed from its predecessors in printing poetical passages in the Old Testament as poetry and in grouping verses into paragraphs according to sense units.

The New Testament was published in 1881, the Old Testament in 1885. The work occupied the New Testament translators for about 40 days each year for ten years, while the Old Testament group was occupied for 792 days over a period of 14 years. The revisers gave their time and labour without charge. When they had completed their work, they disbanded. Although the new version was widely accepted (three million copies being sold within the first year) it did not meet with immediate approval. Though not part of the original project, the Apocrypha was published in 1895.

# Out of the mouths of babes …

Ken Taylor's remarkable work for God began with a grumble from one of his ten children.

After supper one evening he gathered his children around him for the family's nightly Bible reading. And, as usual, he had to 'translate' the chosen passage from the family Bible, which was the King James Version. It was the only way he could be sure of retaining his children's interest.

Then, in exasperation, one of the younger children piped up: 'Well, if that's what it means, why doesn't it say so?' This confirmed to Taylor, then a 37-year-old publishing company director, that the problem which his children had with the King James Version was probably universal. It disturbed him that the early English language was doubtless preventing countless children from understanding God's Word.

When travelling between his suburban home and his Chicago office, Taylor used to pass the time by preparing a 'translation' and explanatory notes in readiness for the family's Bible reading. Now he was suddenly struck by an idea: instead of a word-for-word translation, why not a thought-for-thought interpretation?

That evening, Taylor opened his King James Bible and came to

2 Timothy 4:2: 'Preach the word; be instant in season, out of season; reprove, rebuke, exhort with all long suffering and doctrine.'

He interpreted it to read: 'Preach the Word of God urgently at all times, whenever you get the chance, in season and out, when it is convenient and when it is not. Correct and rebuke your people when they need it, encourage them to do right, and all the time be feeding them patiently with God's Word. '

In the months ahead, he used the 45-minute commuter trip to his office to paraphrase the New Testament epistles. Spurred on by his child's cheeky question, he became increasingly convinced that he could fill a large gap in the Christian family book market.

It was the start of a remarkable 17-year mission which was to begin with his interpretation of the epistles, and was finally to end in 1971 with a full interpretation of the King James Version. It was entitled *The Living Bible*.

The number of complete English-language editions of Kenneth Taylor's paraphrase, *The Living Bible*, printed up to 1996, exceeded 40 million. The text of *The Living Bible* has now been thoroughly revised as the *New Living Translation*, published in 1996.

# Bizarre Bibles

A number of editions and printings of
the Bible have contained curious
translations or errors. As a result
several Bibles have gained special
names. These include:

### The Breeches Bible
The Geneva Bible (1560), so called
because Genesis 3:7 reads, 'They
sewed fig tree leaves together, and
made themselves breeches.

### The Bug Bible
Coverdale's Bible
(1535), so called because Psalm 91:5
reads, 'Thou shalt not need to be
afraid for any bugs by night.' The
Authorized (King James) Version has
'terror by night'.

### The Discharge Bible
An early 19th-
century edition that has 'discharge'
instead of 'charge' in 1 Timothy 5:21
– 'I discharge thee before God.'

### The Ears to Ear Bible
An 1810
printing in which Matthew 13:43
reads, 'Who hath ears to ear, let him
hear.' The Authorized (King James)
Version has 'ears to *hear*'.

### The Fool Bible
A 17th-century
printing that substituted 'a' for 'no' in
Psalm 14:1 – 'The fool hath said in
his heart there is a God.' The printers
were fined £3,000 for this error.

### The He Bible and the She Bible
Two
versions of the Authorized (King
James) Bible (1611), with different
translations of Ruth 3:15. In the He
Bible the verse reads, 'He went into
the city'; in the She Bible, 'She went
into the city.' The NIV gives 'he' in
the text (marginal note: 'Most
Hebrew manuscripts') and 'she' in the
margin ('many Hebrew manuscripts,
Vulgate and Syriac she').

### The Murderers' Bible
An edition
of 1801 in which 'murderers' was
substituted for 'murmurers' in
Jude 16.

### The Place-makers' Bible
The second
edition of the Geneva Bible (1562),
which misprints for Matthew 5:9 as
'Blessed are the place-makers' instead
of 'Blessed are the peacemakers.'

### The Printers' Bible
An edition of
about 1702 that has 'printers' instead
of 'princes' in Psalm 119:161 –
'Printers have persecuted me without
a cause.'

### The Rebecca's Camels Bible
An
edition printed in 1823 that has for
Genesis 24:61, 'Rebecca arose, and
her camels' – this should read
'damsels' instead of 'camels'

**The Rosin Bible** The Douai Bible (1609), so called because of its translation of Jeremiah 8:22, 'Is there no rosin in Gilead?'

**The Standing Fishes Bible** A printing of 1806 that has for Ezekiel 47:10, 'And it shall come to pass, that the fishes shall stand upon it.' 'Fishes' should be 'fishers'.

**The To Remain Bible** A printing of 1805 in which Galatians 4:29 reads, '… persecuted him that was born after the spirit to remain, even so it is not.' The words 'to remain' were the answer to a proof-reader's query concerning the comma after 'spirit', and were mistakenly included by the compositor. The mistake was repeated in the first octavo edition published by the Bible Society (1805) and also in the duodecimo edition of 1819.

**The Treacle Bible** The Bishops' Bible (1568), so called because Jeremiah 8:22 reads, 'Is there no treacle in Gilead?'

**The Unrighteous Bible** An edition printed in 1653 that contains a printer's error in 1 Corinthians 6:9 – 'Know ye not that the unrighteous shall inherit the kingdom of God?' 'Shall inherit' should be 'shall not inherit'.

**The Vinegar Bible** An edition printed in 1717 with the heading for Luke 20, 'The Parable of the Vinegar' instead of 'The Parable of the Vineyard'.

**The Wicked Bible** An edition printed in 1632 that omitted the word 'not' in the seventh commandment (Exodus 20:14), the printed version being 'Thou shalt commit adultery.'

**The Wife-hater Bible** An edition printed in 1810 in which the word 'life' in Luke 14:26 ('If any man come to me, and hate not … his own life also') was printed as 'wife'.

# The 20th century: a multiplicity of versions

Until recent years the Authorized (King James) Version has reigned supreme in the English-speaking world. The wording of this version has become part of the very fabric of the English language (see Section 2,

# The main 20th-century English translations

1903: Richard F. Weymouth, *The New Testament in Modern Speech*. A literary translation.

---

1913, 1924: James Moffatt, *A New Translation of the Bible*. A modern idiomatic translation.

---

1937: Charles B. Williams, *The New Testament in the Language of the People*. A translation that attempts a precise rendering of Greek tenses.

---

1941, 1949: Samuel Henry Hooke, *The Bible in Basic English*. A translation using a very restricted vocabulary.

---

1944, 1949: Ronald A. Knox, *The Holy Bible*. A Roman Catholic translation based on the Latin Vulgate.

---

1946, 1952: *Revised Standard Version (The Common Bible)* (New Testament 2nd edition, 1971). A revision of the American Standard Version (1901); a widely used translation with the aim of retaining the classic English style of the Authorized (King James) Version and considering modern scholarship.

---

1958, 1962: *Amplified Bible*. An 'expanded' translation that gives synonyms to render the original.

---

1958: J. B. Phillips, *The New Testament in Modern English* (2nd edition, 1972). A free, very readable translation.

---

1961, 1970: *New English Bible*. A completely new translation produced by an interdenominational team of British scholars; a dignified, formal style.

---

1963: *New American Standard Bible*. A revision of the American Standard Version prepared by evangelical scholars; a close and conservative translation.

---

1966: *The Jerusalem Bible*. A scholarly, widely appreciated Roman Catholic translation from original texts; based on work by members of the Dominican *Ecole Biblique* of Jerusalem.

1966, 1976: *Good News Bible* (*Today's English Version*) (Revised 1994). An easy-to-read translation in straightforward English, prepared by the American Bible Society.

1969: William Barclay, *New Translation*. A straightforward translation of the New Testament in modern English.

1970: *The New American Bible* (New Testament revised, 1987). A modern Roman Catholic translation from the original languages sponsored by the Bishops' Committee of the Confraternity of Christian Doctrine.

1971: Kenneth N. Taylor, *The Living Bible*. A modern colloquial paraphrase.

1973, 1978: *New International Version* (Revised, 1984). A conservative translation into contemporary English by an international team of evangelical scholars.

1979, 1982: *New King James Version/Revised Authorized Version*. A revision of the *Authorized (King James) Version*, with archaic and obsolete words and meanings modernized.

1985: *New Jerusalem Bible*. An extensive revision of the *Jerusalem Bible*.

1989: *Revised English Bible*. A far-reaching revision of the *New English Bible*; the result of cooperation between Protestant and Roman Catholic churches.

1990: *New Revised Standard Version*. A revision of the *Revised Standard Version*, including some gender-inclusive language.

1994: *The Message*. A very lively paraphrase of the New Testament in contemporary American English.

1995: *Contemporary English Version*. A fresh translation designed particularly to be read aloud and listened to easily.

1996: *New Living Translation*. A thorough revision of the *Living Bible*, emphasizing 'thought-for-thought' translation.

## What hath God wrought

The words, 'What hath God wrought' (Numbers 23:23, AV) were the first words to be sent by electromagnetic telegraph. The message was sent by Samuel F. B. Morse over a 40-mile line between Washington DC and Baltimore, Maryland on 24th May 1844.

'And this Good News about the Kingdom will be preached through all the world for a witness to all nations; and then the end will come'

Jesus, in Matthew 24:14 (GNB)

pages 45f). If verses were learnt, they were learnt in this version.

In the 20th century there have been many new translations (and paraphrases) intended not only to translate the original text accurately, but also to express its meaning in contemporary language.

# Bible translation: the unfinished task

## Why can't God speak my language?

'If your God is so great, why can't he speak my language?' Those words struck young Cameron Townsend hard. It was 1918. Cameron had come to Guatemala to sell Bibles. But the Bibles were all in Spanish, and as this man pointed out, Spanish wasn't his language. Why couldn't God speak Cakchiquel?

'Ah, but he can', thought Cameron. 'He can and he must, if this man and others like him are to understand his message.'

So Cameron laid aside the Spanish Bibles and went with his wife to live among the Cakchiquel. He learned their language and their culture. He established churches and schools. But the heart of his programme was the translation of God's Word into Cakchiquel, the only language that really spoke to the hearts of these people.

That Word bore fruit. One man whom Cameron taught to read bought a New Testament simply because there wasn't much else to read in Cakchiquel. He was a leader in the tribal religion, but one day he announced to his people, 'I want to believe in Christ.' The idols that crowded his home disappeared soon after that. The new convert said, 'Listen, I served them all my life. I thought it was time they served me, so I made kindling wood out of them and cooked my beans.'

## The Biscuit-tin Bible

A Bible in the Ganda language (or Luganda, spoken in Uganda) published in 1896 has a curiously squat appearance. Its shape gave rise to the legend that the British and Foreign Bible Society had produced it to fit into the tin biscuit boxes which were commonly used by the people for holding books, and it became known as the 'Biscuit-tin Bible'. In fact, the shape was due to the fact that the separate portions were bound up in their original form without resetting, to meet the urgent need for a complete Bible.

# The caring comma

'And his gifts were that some should be apostles, some prophets, some evangelists, some pastors and teachers, for the equipment of the saints, for the work of ministry, for building up the body of Christ.' So reads Ephesians 4:11–12 in the first edition of the Revised Standard Version. The second edition of its New Testament has the same text, except that 'for the equipment of the saints, for the work of ministry' is replaced by 'to equip the saints for the work of ministry'.

The wording of the original edition (in common with the Authorized (King James) Version) suggested that the work of the special ministers was threefold: (1) equipping the saints, (2) the work of the ministry and (3) building up the body of Christ. The revised edition (in common with other newer translations) suggests that their work is two-fold: (1) equipping the saints for the work of ministry and (2) building up the body of Christ. The dropping of a comma creates a wording which implies that it is not the special ministers who do the work of ministry and so build up the body of Christ; it is 'the saints' themselves – all Christians – who exercise the work of ministry as a result of their being equipped by the special ministers.

Cameron Townsend began to dream of God's Word being translated into the many local languages in Brazil, Mexico, Africa, China and throughout the world. Today, many people are working in different language areas to make that dream come true, to make God's Word understood by all people, everywhere.

# Getting down to it

Often the translator has to begin by:
• Developing an alphabet that corresponds to the sounds of the language.
• Building up a vocabulary.
• Distinguishing grammatical structure.
• Getting the right meaning across to a particular culture.
• Discovering the appropriate idioms and metaphors.

The last two items present many problems. How, for instance, do you translate 'fig tree' for Eskimos, who have never seen one? Or 'lamb of God' for people who have never seen a sheep? Or 'white as snow' for the people of Tonga? In this case 'white as a flock of egrets' was used.

Then there are different customs. For the Bambara people of Mali and

Burkina Faso, snakes form a specially appetizing and acceptable part of their diet. The translation of 'Or would you give him a snake when he asks for a fish?' (Matthew 7:10) needs careful thought if the meaning is to be made plain!

Even more difficult is the translation of essentially biblical terms such as 'covenant' and 'parable', or of apparently simple words like 'peace' and 'love'. The same word may need varying translations in different parts of the Bible if the original message is to come through to people.

## 'We are now part of the world'

In 1983 Wycliffe Bible Translators announced the completion of the 200th New Testament translation in which their members had been involved. It was the Hanga New Testament, the work of a team in Ghana led by British members Geoffrey and Rosemary Hunt. The Hanga language is spoken by several thousand people living in a dozen villages in northern Ghana. The Hanga New Testament was the fruit of the cooperative efforts of many people and organizations. It would not have been possible without the capable work of several Hanga people.

Geoffrey and Rosemary took up residence in the Hanga village of Langantere in 1971 in order to learn the language and carry out Bible translation. This work was initiated under the auspices of the Summer Institute of Linguistics, an organization affiliated to the Wycliffe Bible Translators. Since 1980 the work in Ghana has been administered by the Ghana Institute of Linguistics, Literacy and Bible Translation. This is an organization of Ghanaian Christians who share the conviction that all people deserve to have the Bible in their own language.

> 'You are worthy to take the scroll and to break open its seals. For you were killed, and by your sacrificial death you bought for God people from *every tribe, language, nation and race*.'
> Revelation 5:9, emphasis added (GNB)

Here are some of the things that happened once the Hanga people had the New Testament in their own language:

## The literacy work bore fruit

People in some Hanga villages quickly began meeting together to have the New Testament read aloud. The literacy supervisors were asked to explain

# A very important city

In the book of Jonah you have a 'great' city, Nineveh. It, of course, had been excavated and we knew the exact size. But when the Bible, in another place talks of Gibeon as a 'great' city using the same Hebrew word, *gadol*, one begins to examine what was the purpose of this designation. Gibeon has been excavated. It's a small area. We find the word 'great' means it's an important administrative centre. And the book of Jonah talks about the size of Nineveh. Most translations said it took three days to walk through it. Archaeology questioned that. We used to ride around the walls of Nineveh, which is only nine and a quarter miles going all the way around the walls. In the New International Version we examined the old customs which were mentioned in modern and ancient texts. We saw that 'of three days' means that it's an important administrative city where, as you do in Bedonin Arab custom, you have to stay overnight. In other words, the

first day you arrive. The next day you do your business, and the third day you're up and away.

The Authorized (King James) Version leaves the reader with the wrong impression when it says (Jonah 3:3) 'Now Nineveh was an exceeding great city of three days' journey.' Thanks to archaeology, the meaning comes through clearly in the New International Version: 'Now Nineveh was a very important city – a visit required three days.'
(Donald J. Wiseman, *A Bible for Today and Tomorrow*, Hodder and Stoughton)

passages which were not understood. A chief actually asked to be taught to read so that he would not have to 'disturb' the young men in his village by asking them to come and read to him. Having a young man teach a chief was not traditional, but he was willing to break with tradition in this matter. Other leading men responded positively too. One very old chief said, 'Since this book came to us and we can read it, *we are now part of the world.*'

## People became Christians

One man was so excited with the New Testament that he wanted to go to other villages to preach the gospel right away. David, a more mature Christian, wisely suggested that he remained in his own village and

learned to live as a Christian there first. He could share with others how he 'used Jesus every day'. Another Hanga man, who presumably had only recently learned to read, quickly got as far as Matthew 25, and wrote: 'I pray that the Hanga people will be like the five wise virgins, ready for Jesus Christ.' Untaught, he had understood not just the surface meaning but the deeper meaning too, and had acted upon it.

## The church grew

Although the people gladly welcomed the New Testament, the changes that Christ brought in people's lives were not necessarily so welcome. One man from a Muslim background came across statements in the New

# Statistics on Bible translation up to 1997

- At present, a total of at least 6,500 languages are currently spoken in the world.
- Of these, 2,123 languages have some or all of the Bible (349 complete Bibles, 841 New Testaments).
- Languages needing Bible translation: an estimated 2,500 – 3,000, representing over 300 million people.
- Population of each language group: varies greatly from less than 100 to several million.

- Time required to translate the New Testament: About 15 years – sometimes a lot more, occasionally less. The progress of translation is assisted by adequate preparation and training, on-the-field consultation and workshops, the availability of technical helps, computer-editing, and partnership with the local community.

Testament that contradicted his Islamic faith. One thing that kept him searching was John 14:6, 'I am the way, the truth and the life. Anyone is not able to reach my Father God's place, unless I have him go.' He had never heard of Mohammed making such a claim. Finally he gave up his Muslim way of worship and became a dedicated follower of Jesus Christ. He was thrown out of his father's house when he attended a Bible training course.

By 1989 there were about 100 Christians among the Hanga people. 'The people who were No People are becoming My People.'

# The Bible and the English Language

## Bible quotations

Quotations from the Authorized (King James) Version of the Bible have become well established in the English language. We speak, often without realizing the biblical origins of the phrases we are using, of 'the salt of the earth', of 'the powers that be' or of escaping something 'by the skin of our teeth'. We allude to biblical stories when we refer to 'the writing on the wall' and 'the prodigal son'. And at times we even misquote Scripture when we say such things as 'money is the root of all evil'. Here is a selection of phrases that have become part of the language. (All quotations in this section are, unless otherwise stated, from the Authorized (King James) Version.)

BREAK GLASS IN CASE OF FIRE

(OR BRIMSTONE)

## The Old Testament

The expression '**forbidden fruit**', sometimes with the additional phrase,

'**is** (or **tastes**) **sweetest**', means something which is desired because it is not allowed or approved of. The phrase alludes to Eve's eating the fruit of the tree of the knowledge of good and evil (Genesis 3:1–7).

To be '**one's brother's keeper**' means that one accepts responsibility for someone's behaviour or well-being. The phrase comes from Genesis 4:9, 'Am I my brother's keeper?', the reply of Cain to the Lord after Cain had killed his brother Abel.

The expression, '**fire and brimstone**' means punishment and destruction that is inflicted by God. In the original reference to the punishment meted out on Sodom and Gomorrah (Genesis 19:24), the words 'fire' and 'brimstone' are reversed. In other biblical references (e.g. Psalm 11:6, Luke 17:29 and Revelation 20:10), the familiar order of 'fire' and 'brimstone' is retained.

The phrase, '**the fat years and the lean years**' refers to times of success and hardship in the life of a person, country or business: 'It looks like the company's fat years are over and we'll have to cope with the lean for a while to come.' The expression alludes to Joseph's interpretation of Pharaoh's dream (Genesis 41:25–7).

'**A land flowing with milk and honey**' is a place or condition that offers abundant fulfilment of one's hopes and great happiness. The expression comes from Exodus 3:8, describing the 'promised land' (see also Genesis 12:5–8), the land of Canaan promised by the Lord to the Israelites.

'**An eye for an eye, and a tooth for a tooth**' means retaliation that is expressed in the same way as the

# The first shibboleth

A shibboleth is a use of language or a saying or custom, especially one that distinguishes members of a certain group. The origin of the word lies in Judges 12:4–6. In a battle between the Gileadites and Ephraimites, the Gileadites captured the fords. When any of the Ephraimite survivors wanted to cross, they would be asked if they were Ephraimites. If the answer was no, they would then be asked to say the word shibboleth. Because of their Ephraimite accent, they would pronounce the word as *sibboleth*. Anyone who gave the incorrect pronunciation of *shibboleth* was killed.

offence that was committed. The phrase comes from Exodus 21:24 and also from Jesus' Sermon on the Mount (Matthew 5:38).

'**The apple of one's eye**' is a person whom one treasures as precious. The phrase comes from Deuteronomy 32:10', 'He kept him as the apple of his eye,' which refers to the Lord's love for Israel. The apple was a metaphor for the pupil of the eye, since an apple and a pupil were both round. The association of the eye – itself very highly valued – with someone who is cherished lies behind this expression.

'**A man after one's own heart**' is a person who is exactly of the kind that one likes most, because they have the same inner disposition and interests as oneself. The source of the expression is 1 Samuel 13:14, 'The LORD hath sought him a man after his own heart'. God was looking for someone who would closely follow his ways.

To '**gird up one's loins**' is to prepare for energetic action. This rather old-fashioned idiomatic expression, which

first appears in the Bible in 1 Kings 18:46, comes from the Israelites' wearing of loose, flowing robes. These were impractical for working or travelling in unless they were fastened by a girdle or belt. So when Elijah 'girded up his loins' ('tucking his cloak into his belt' NIV) he was preparing for the difficult task that was about to be faced.

The expression '**a still, small voice**' is sometimes used in modern English to stand for the 'voice' of one's conscience, one's inner sense of right and wrong. The phrase comes from 1 Kings 19:12, describing the quite gentle way in which the LORD spoke to Elijah after he had fled to Horeb.

The phrase, '**sackcloth and ashes**' refers to the custom of wearing a garment of rough woven cloth and of scattering ashes over one's head and body as a sign of mourning or repentance. The expression, first used in Esther 4:3, is used several times in the Old and New Testaments in a literal sense, and is now used figuratively to describe sorrow for one's wrong actions. (Ash Wednesday, the first day of Lent, is so named from the practice of sprinkling ashes on the heads of penitents.)

To '**escape by the skin of one's teeth**' means to escape something narrowly.

# My cup shall be full

A number of phrases and expressions that have become a familiar part of the language derive from Miles Coverdale's translation of the Psalms, as found in the Book of Common Prayer. These expressions include:

- **'my cup shall be full'**, from Psalm 23:5
- **'flourish like a green bay-tree'**, from Psalm 37:35
- **'the iron entered into his soul'** from Psalm 105:18
- **'at death's door'**, from Psalm 107:18
- **'high-minded'**, from Psalm 131:1

The expression comes from Job 19:20, 'I am escaped with the skin of my teeth.'

The comment, **'Out of the mouths of babes and sucklings ...'** is sometimes said when a young child makes a wise and perceptive remark. It comes from Psalm 8:2, originally referring to the praise of God. Derek Kidner translates it as, 'from the cradle and the nursery' (*Psalms: An introduction and Commentary*, Inter-Varsity Press).

Psalm 23 is among the best-known parts of the Bible and a number of idiomatic expressions derive from it: **'the valley of the shadow of death'** (verse 4), the dark circumstances in which one finds oneself facing death; **'one's cup runneth over'** (verse 5), one has full joys; **'all the days of one's life'** (verse 6)', for as long as one lives.

To '**go from strength to strength**' is to become more and more successful: 'What with all these new contracts coming in, the business is really going from strength to strength.' The phrase comes from Psalm 84:7, 'They go from strength to strength, every one of them in Zion appeareth before God.'

**'Three score years and ten'** is seventy years, the period of time that people may be expected to live; they may live **four score** or eighty years, if given the strength. The expressions derive from Psalm 90:10. Interestingly, the original Hebrew has simply 'seventy' and 'eighty'.

Two proverbial expressions allude to verses in the book of Proverbs. The saying, **'Spare the rod and spoil the child'** used to support physical punishment, alludes to Proverbs 13:24, 'He that spareth his rod hateth his son: but he that loveth him chasteneth him betimes', and to Proverbs 23:13–14, 'Withhold not correction from the child: for if thou beatest him with the rod, he shall not die. Thou shalt beat him with the rod, and shalt deliver his soul from hell.' The saying, **'Pride goes before a fall'**, which means that someone who is over-confident is soon likely to suffer misfortune, alludes to Proverbs 16:18, 'Pride goeth before destruction, and an haughty spirit before a fall.'

The expression, **'There is nothing new under the sun'** is applied to something that looks original and novel but in fact is not. It comes originally from Ecclesiastes 1:9, 'There is no new thing under the sun.'

**'There's a time and a place for everything'** means that there are certain circumstances when a particular action is appropriate. It is often used with the implication that a particular action may not be done at any time or in any place. The origin of the expression lies in the Preacher's statement of the different times and seasons of human existence, as recorded in Ecclesiastes 3:1–8.

The saying, **'Eat, drink and be merry'**, sometimes followed by **'for tomorrow we die'**, expresses the philosophy that worldly pleasures should be enjoyed fully at the present time, because the future is uncertain. The phrase is derived from Ecclesiastes 8:15 and Isaiah 22:13.

**'A fly in the ointment'** is a person or thing that spoils a situation that is perfect in every other way: 'The only fly in the ointment was the poor weather; otherwise the fete went very well indeed.' The expression comes from Ecclesiastes 10:1, 'Dead flies cause the ointment of the apothecary to send forth a stinking savour.' As dead flies give even sweet-smelling perfume a bad odour, so a little folly outweighs the good qualities of wisdom and honour.

'**A drop in the ocean**' (or '**bucket**') is something which is very small in comparison with something much larger that is required. The expression derives from Isaiah 40:15, 'Behold, the nations are as a drop of a bucket' – the nations of the world are insignificant when compared with the greatness of God.

'**A word in season**' is used to describe advice or warning given at the right time. The phrase comes from Isaiah 50:4, which is part of one of the 'Servant Songs' – 'The Lord God hath given me the tongue of the learned, that I should know how to speak a word in season to him that is weary.'

The expression, '**like a lamb** (or **sheep**) **to the slaughter**' means quietly and without complaining. It is often used to refer to someone who is unwittingly about to go into a dangerous or difficult situation or to be the helpless victim of punishment. The basis of the expression is Isaiah 53:7, 'he is brought as a lamb to the slaughter and as a sheep before her shearers is dumb, so he openeth not his mouth', and Acts 8:32, where the prophecy is applied to Jesus.

The saying, '**there is no peace for the wicked**' is sometimes used ironically as a mild comment when one is under pressure or has to do something that one does not want to do. The expression comes originally from Isaiah 57:21, which implies that anxiety and fear are experienced by those who do evil.

People who are '**holier-than-thou**' behave towards others in a way that shows that they think they are more moral or virtuous than them. The origin of this phrase lies in Isaiah 65:5, which says, 'Stand by thyself, come not near to me; for I am holier than thou'. Isaiah was prophesying against some who smugly claimed to be more righteous than others.

The expression, '**The leopard cannot change his spots**' means that one cannot change one's basic human character; one has to act according to one's nature. The saying comes from Jeremiah 13:23, 'Can the Ethiopian

# ... And from the Apocrypha

A number of phrases that have passed into the language come from the text of the Apocrypha. These include:

- **'Let us now praise famous men'**, from Ecclesiasticus 44:1
- **'a Daniel come to judgment'** used to refer to an upright person who makes a wise decision about something that has puzzled others.

The expression alludes to the Daniel of the Old Testament and the apocryphal History of Susanna. The source of the phrase itself is Shakespeare's *Merchant of Venice* (Act 4, Scene 1).

- **'at the** (or **one's**) **last gasp'**, at the point of death or collapse, from 2 Maccabees 7:9

change his skin, or the leopard his spots?'

The phrase, **'wheels within wheels'** describes a complex set of inter-connected influences or issues. The origin of the expression is in Ezekiel's vision of the living creatures and the glory of God: 'And they four had one likeness: and their appearance and their work was as it were a wheel in the middle of a wheel' (Ezekiel 1:16).

Someone is said to have **'feet of clay'** when, although being a person who is respected, he or she has a fundamental and usually hidden weakness. The expression comes from Daniel 2:33, where the statue seen in Nebuchadnezzar's dream is described: it had a head made of gold, a chest and arms of silver, a belly and thighs of bronze, legs of iron and feet of iron and clay. The feet, according to

Daniel's explanation, were struck by a stone which broke them to pieces and so smashed the rest of the statue. Thus *feet of clay* in modern usage means a vulnerable or weak point.

The expression, **'the writing on the wall'** refers to signs that warn of imminent failure or ruin: 'They've seen the writing on the wall and know that they'll lose their jobs before Christmas.' The phrase alludes to the mysterious inscription that appeared on the wall of the royal palace of King Belshazzar (Daniel 5), which was interpreted as describing the king's downfall. One of the words inscribed was *Tekel*, interpreted by Daniel as referring to King Belshazzar's life, which had been **'weighed in the balances'** and **'found wanting'** (verse 27). This expression has also passed into the language and means that someone or something has been judged and is considered not to meet the required standard.

The phrase, '**the law of the Medes and the Persians**' means an established rule or practice that has to be followed rigidly: 'It's not a law of the Medes and the Persians, is it, that we have to have tea at six o'clock every day?' The expression comes from Daniel 6:8 – 'Now, O king, establish the decree, and sign the writing, that it be not changed, according to the law of the Medes and Persians, which altereth not.' This was the call of the administrators who went to King Darius with the idea of issuing an edict that anyone who prayed to any god or man except the king in the following 30 days should be thrown into the lion's den. When King Cyrus controlled Media in 550 BC, the traditions and laws of Media were joined to those of the Persians. (see also Daniel 6:15; Esther 1:19.)

The expression, '**Sow the wind and reap the whirlwind**' means to do something that appears harmless but leads to the suffering of unforeseen disastrous consequences. The source of this phrase lies in Hosea 8:7 – Israel had sown the wind of idolatry and would reap the whirlwind of an Assyrian invasion.

# The New Testament

The phrase, '**a voice crying in the wilderness**' is used to describe someone who is speaking out a warning or giving advice which the public ignore: 'For years she was a voice crying in the wilderness – constantly issuing unheeded warnings about the danger to the environment.' The expression derives from Matthew 3:3 and describes John the Baptist: 'The voice of one crying in the wilderness, Prepare ye the way of the LORD, make his paths straight.'

Jesus' Sermon on the Mount (Matthew 5–7) has given the language a large number of phrases and expressions including the following:
- '**the salt of the earth**' – people thought to have an admirable character and to be of great value (5:13).
- '**hide one's light under a bushel**' – to conceal or be too modest about one's abilities or talents (5:15).
- '**a jot or tittle**' – the smallest part (5:18).
- '**turn the other cheek**' – to refuse to retaliate when provoked; sometimes also to be ready to be humiliated again (5:39)
- '**one's left hand does not know what one's right hand is doing**' – applied, for example, to lack of

communication between departments or disorganized work methods in large institutions (6:3).

- 'one's daily bread' – the food and other necessities that one requires in order to live (6:11).
- 'serve God and mammon' – to be devoted to both spiritual and worldly (especially money) matters (6:24).
- 'the beam in one's own eye (and the mote in someone else's eye)' – a serious fault in one's own nature or opinions which one iguores while criticizing unimportant faults in other people (7:3).
- 'cast pearls before swine' – to waste something valuable on those who cannot appreciate it (7:6).
- 'a wolf in sheep's clothing' – someone who appears friendly and harmless but in reality is cruel and dangerous (7:15).

The expression, 'say the word' means to state one's wishes to someone who is willing to fulfil them immediately: 'Just say the word and I'll come'. The phrase derives from Matthew 8:8, 'The centurion answered and said, Lord, I am not worthy that thou shouldest come under my roof: but speak the word only, and my servant shall be healed.'

The phrase, 'gnashing of teeth' means to grind one's upper and lower teeth together forcefully in anger or pain. It comes from Matthew 8:12, 'The children of the kingdom shall be cast out into outer darkness: there shall be weeping and gnashing of teeth.'

The expression, 'shake the dust off one's feet' is sometimes used to mean departing from a place angrily because one has not been well treated there. The quotation comes from Matthew 8:14, 'And whosoever shall not receive you, nor hear your words, when ye depart out of that house or city, shake off the dust of your feet.' For an example of this, see Acts 13:50–51.

To 'fall by the wayside' is to give up or to fail in an activity because of weakness: 'The course started out with 60 students, but quite a number seem to have fallen by the wayside'. The phrase comes from the parable of the sower and the seed in Matthew 13:4, 'some seeds fell by the way side.'

The saying, '**A prophet is without honour in his own country**' is nowadays applied to someone who is recognized as great by everyone except his own family, compatriots, etc. The expression is derived from Jesus' words in Matthew 14:57, 'A prophet is not without honour, save in his own country, and in his own house.'

The phrase, '**the blind leading the blind**' is sometimes used to describe the situation when inexperienced people try to guide others who are similarly inexperienced. The saying derives from Jesus' description of the Pharisees in Matthew 15:14, 'Let them alone: they be blind leaders of the blind. And if the blind lead the blind, both shall fall into the ditch.'

'**At the eleventh hour**' means 'at the last minute' – 'Thankfully, we managed to find a replacement at the eleventh hour'. The phrase comes from Jesus' parable of the workers in the vineyard (Matthew 20:1–16). The workers hired at the eleventh hour received the same pay as those who had been hired earlier.

## Maundy Thursday

Maundy Thursday is the name given to the Thursday before Easter, which commemorates Christ's Last Supper with his disciples. The name comes from the Old French word *mandé*, meaning 'commanded'; this word in turn comes from the Latin *mandatum*, or 'commandment', which occurs in the Latin translation of Christ's words in John 13:43, '*Mandatum novum do vobis*' – 'A new commandment I give unto you.' This new commandment was 'that ye love one another as I have loved you,' and had been shown by Jesus' washing of his disciples' feet.

Tradition has it that on Maundy Thursday the reigning British monarch presents specially minted coins to a number of elderly people (one man and one woman for each year of his or her life) in a chosen cathedral city. Originally the monarch washed the feet of a few poor people and then distributed food and clothes, but the former custom fell into abeyance and the latter was replaced by the giving of money.

'**The chosen few**' means a comparatively small group of people who are in a favoured position: 'I expect it's just the chosen few who are invited, as usual.' The expression comes from Matthew 20:16, 'For many be called, but few chosen.'

'**A den of thieves**' is a meeting-place used as a hide-out by thieves or rogues. The phrase derives from Matthew 21:13, 'It is written, My house shall be called the house of prayer; but ye have made it a den of thieves.'

Jesus' denunciation of the Pharisees in Matthew 23 contains a number of expressions which have become part of the language, including **strain at a gnat** (and **swallow a camel**), which means to be very concerned about insignificant matters that are wrong while ignoring those matters what are really important (23:24). Another expression found here is whited sepulchres, which means hypocrites, those who pretend to be righteous when in reality they are not (23:27).

The expression, '**The spirit is willing but the flesh is weak**' is used to suggest that someone lacks the ability, energy or will-power to put his or her good intentions into practice. The phrase derives from Matthew 26:41, where Jesus warns his disciples to

remain alert and not to yield to temptation.

To '**wash one's hands of something**' means to say or show that one no longer wishes to be responsible for or involved in an action: 'They wanted to wash their hands of the whole sordid affair.' This idiomatic phrase has its origins in Matthew 27:24. Pilate washed his hands, symbolizing his dissociation from the desire of the people to crucify Jesus. He refused to assume responsibility for Jesus' death.

If something '**falls on stony ground**', it is not received or listened to – 'The idea of expanding broadcasting of the arts fell on stony ground and was quickly abandoned.' The expression derives from Mark 4:5–6, from the parable of the sower and the seed; 'And some fell on stony ground, where it had not much earth; and immediately it sprang up, because it had no depth of earth: But when the sun was up, it was scorched; and because it had no root, it withered away.'

The saying, '**The labourer is worthy of his hire**' means that someone in another person's employment should receive fair payment for the work which he or she has done. The expression derives from Jesus' words in Luke 10:7.

A '**good Samaritan**' is someone who unselfishly helps a person who is in distress or difficulty. The term comes fromJesus' parable in Luke 10:30–37. Nowadays the good Samaritan is sometimes remembered in connection with this remark made by the British prime minister Margaret Thatcher: 'No one would remember the Good Samaritan if he'd only had good intentions. He had money as well.' The expression, '**pass by on the other side**', meaning to give no help or sympathy to someone in need, derives from the actions of the priest and the Levite in this parable (verses 31–32).

A '**prodigal**' or a '**prodigal son**' is a reformed spendthrift – for example, someone who leaves the family home as a youth and wastes all his money, but later returns home, sorry for his actions. The expression alludes to the parable of Jesus, recorded in Luke 15:11–32. When the son returned he was welcomed home by his father, who celebrated his homecoming by holding a feast. They '**killed the fatted calf**' in his honour – they gave him the best possible food and treatment.

The phrase, '**born again**' is sometimes used in contemporary English to describe an enthusiastic conversion to a particular cause (for example, a 'born-again monetarist');
or it may be used as a synonym for 'renewed', 'fresh' or 'new'. The origin of the expression is Jesus' explanation to Nicodemus in John 3:5–7. Unless Nicodemus was reborn spiritually – was radically changed by the Spirit of God in his inner being – he could not enter the kingdom of God.

The expression, '**no respecter of persons**' describes an attitude in which everyone involved is dealt with in the same way, regardless of their wealth, rank, and so on: 'The plague was no respecter of persons – in their millions young and old, rich and poor, famous and unknown, perished as the epidemic swept across the continent.' The phrase derives from Acts 10:34, where Peter says to Cornelius and his relatives and close friends that God 'has no favourites', and that his grace is extended to Gentiles as freely as it is extended to Jews.

To be '**a law unto oneself**' means that one does what one wants and sets one's moral guidelines, without taking into account the usual conventions of society or the advice of others. The expression derives from Romans 2:14 – 'For when the Gentiles, which have not the law, do by nature the things contained in the law, these, having not the law, are a law unto themselves.'

# Who said it?

Who said these words and on what occasion? The answers appear below.

1. 'Let my people go.'
2. 'Sufficient unto the day is the evil thereof.'
3. 'Physician, heal thyself.'
4. 'I have been a stranger in a strange land.'
5. 'How are the mighty fallen.'
6. 'And he shall rule them with a rod of iron.'
7. 'Woe is me! … I am a man of unclean lips …'
8. 'Let them be hewers of wood and drawers of water.'
9. 'For who hath despised the day of small things?'
10. 'It is hard for thee to kick against the pricks.'
11. 'Ye shall no more give the people straw to make brick, as heretofore: let them go and gather straw for themselves.'
12. 'Is there no balm in Gilead?'
13. 'Let the dead bury their dead.'
14. 'Can ye not discern the signs of the times?'
15. 'I have played the fool.'

**Answers**

1. Moses and Aaron, saying God's words to Pharaoh (Exodus 5:1).
2. Jesus, advising his hearers not to worry about tomorrow, in the Sermon on the Mount (Matthew 6:34).
3. Jesus, quoting this proverb at his home town of Nazareth (Luke 4:23).
4. Moses, naming his son Gershom (Exodus 2:22). The name sounds like the Hebrew for 'an alien there.'
5. David, in his lament for Saul and Jonathan (2 Samuel 1:19).
6. The words of Jesus to John, to be written to the church in Thyatira (Revelation 2:27).
7. Isaiah, on seeing a vision of the Lord (Isaiah 6:5).
8. The princes (leaders) of Israel, concerning the people of Gibeon, after they had discovered their deception (Joshua 9:21).
9. The word of the Lord to Zechariah concerning the work of rebuilding the temple (Zechariah 4:10).
10. The Lord Jesus to Saul on his way to Damascus (Acts 9:5).
11. Pharaoh, ordering the taskmasters and officers of the people of Israel (Exodus 5:7).
12. Jeremiah on the lack of effective means of healing the hurt of Judah (Jeremiah 8:22).
13. Jesus, describing the implications of discipleship (Matthew 8:22).
14. Jesus, in response to the Pharisees and the Sadducees when they asked for a sign from heaven (Matthew 16:3).
15. Saul to David, after David spared his life (1 Samuel 26:21).

'**The powers that be**' are the controlling authority or governing body of an institution – in other words, the Establishment: 'I hope the powers that be know why so much money is wasted in this organization, because I certainly don't.' This expression comes from Romans 13:1, 'For there is no power but of God: the powers that be are ordained of God.'

People who are '**all things to all men**' try to please everyone, changing their behaviour to suit those with whom they happen to be at any particular time. The phrase is derived from a description of Paul's versatility as

# Money is the root of all evil

Some expressions that are generally thought of as coming from the Bible are in fact inaccurate quotations of the original words. Perhaps the most common biblical misquotation is **'Money is the root of all evil'** from the original, 'the love of money is the root of all evil' (1 Timothy 6:10). Here are some other misquotations:

- **'Esau sold his birthright for a mess of pottage'** from Genesis 25:30–34 and Hebrews 12:16. The words 'mess of' are not in the biblical text.
- **'Go the way of all flesh'** (die or disappear finally) from Joshua 23:14 and 1 Kings 2:2. The Bible text has 'go the way of all the earth'.

- **'A cloud no bigger than a man's hand'** from 1 Kings 18:44. The original has 'Behold, there ariseth a little cloud out of the sea, like a man's hand.'
- **'The lion shall lie down with the lamb'** from Isaiah 11:6, 'The wolf also shall dwell with the lamb, and the leopard shall lie down with the kid; and the calf and the young lion and the fatling together; and a little child shall lead them.'
- **'He that runs may read'** from Habakkuk 2:2, 'Write the vision, and make it plain upon tables, that he may run that readeth it.'

recorded in 1 Corinthians 9:22 – 'To the weak became I as weak, that I might gain the weak; I am made all things to all men, that I might by all means save some.'

If something happens **'in the twinkling of an eye'** it takes place extremely quickly. This expression originates in 1 Corinthians 15:51–52, where Paul the apostle writes, 'We shall all be changed, In a moment, in the twinkling of an eye, at the last trump.'

**'The letter of the law'** is a strict, literal understanding of the law as it is expressed. This phrase is often contrasted with the 'spirit of the law' – that is, the law's general purpose or effect. Both phrases derive from 2 Corinthians 3:5–6, 'God… hath made us able ministers of the new testament; not of the letter, but of the spirit: for the letter killeth, but the spirit giveth life.'

A person who **'does not suffer fools gladly'** is impatient and unsympathetic towards foolish people: 'The former headteacher, never one to suffer fools gladly, dealt very harshly with anyone who attempted to undermine his authority.' The phrase derives from 2 Corinthians 11:19, 'For ye suffer fools gladly, seeing ye yourselves are wise.'

A 'thorn in the flesh (or side)' is a source of constant annoyance: 'The biggest thorn in the association's flesh at the moment is the need to restrict pay increases to just two per cent.' The expression is derived from Paul's description in 2 Corinthians 12:7 of his own experience of such a problem: 'And lest I should be exalted above measure through the abundance of the revelations, there was given to me a thorn in the flesh, the messenger of Satan to buffet me, lest I should be exalted above measure.'

If someone 'falls from grace' he or she loses a privileged or favoured position. The origin of this phrase is Galatians 5:4, 'Christ is become of no effect unto you, whosoever of you are justified by the law; ye are fallen from grace.' The Galatians were trying to put themselves in a right relationship with God by relying on their own efforts to keep the law. They were therefore falling away from receiving God's favour only by grace, and so were rejecting Christ.

If something happens 'like a thief in the night' it comes suddenly and unexpectedly. The phrase derives from 1 Thessalonians 5:2, 'For ye yourselves know perfectly that the day of the Lord so cometh as a thief in the night.'

If something is 'strong meat' it is thought not to be suitable for people who are easily distressed or upset. The expression comes from Hebrews 5:12. The Hebrews needed to be taught again the 'milk' or basic teaching of God's word. They were not yet ready for the 'solid food' which was the more advanced truths.

> 'The English Bible, a book which, if everything else in our language should perish, would alone suffice to show the whole extent of its beauty and power.'
>
> Lord Macaulay, British historian (1800–59)

To '**cover a multitude of sins**' is to deliberately hide many different things, especially faults and weaknesses: 'His job title, "Assistant Adviser", covers a multitude of sins'. The expression originates in 1 Peter 4:8, 'Charity shall cover the multitude of sins.'

The '**alpha and omega**' is the start and end of something, including its most significant aspects. The expression derives from Revelation 1:8, 'I am Alpha and Omega, the beginning and the ending, saith the Lord.'

# Bible names

Do you know what the names Benjamin and Hannah mean? Or how about Matthew, or Mary? In this part of the section we explore personal names derived from the Bible, and we will also look at their meanings and the way they are used in such phrases as '**a doubting Thomas**' and '**the patience of Job**'. There is also a section on place names, used in such expressions as '**in the land of Nod**' and '**a Damascus experience**'.

## First names

This list gives first names that are derived from Bible names, with their meanings.

**Aaron** *possibly* high mountain
**Abel** breath *or* son
**Abigail** father is rejoicing
**Abraham** father of a multitude
**Absalom** father is peace
**Adam** Man *or* of the ground *or* taken out of red earth
**Ahaz** he has grasped
**Amos** carried *or* burden bearer
**Andrew** manly
**Anna** grace

**Aquila** eagle
**Asa** healer
**Asher** happy
**Azariah** Jehovah has helped

**Balaam** devourer
**Barabbas** son of the father *or* teacher
**Barnabas** son of encouragement
**Bartholomew** son of Tamai
**Bathsheba** voluptuous *or* daughter of Eliam/Ammiel
**Belshazzar** may Bel protect the king
**Benjamin** son of my right hand
**Bernice** victorious
**Beulah** married
**Boaz** swiftness

**Cain** possession
**Caleb** dog
**Carmel** garden
**Chloe** green shoot
**Claudia** lame
**Clement** mild, gentle
**Cornelius** of a horn
**Cyrus** sun *or* throne

**Damaris** calf
**Daniel** God is my judge
**David** beloved *or* friend
**Deborah** bee

**Delilah** delight *or* dainty one
**Demetrius** of Demeter, the earth mother
**Dinah** judged
**Dorcas** gazelle
**Drusilla** of the Drusus family

**Ebenezer** stone of help
**Eden** delight
**Eleazar** God is my help
**Eli** high
**Elijah** Jehovah is God
**Elisha** God is salvation
**Elizabeth** oath of God
**Elkanah** God has created
**Emmanuel** God is with us
**Enoch** consecrated *or* trained
**Enos** man
**Ephraim** fruitful
**Esau** hairy
**Esther** star
**Eunice** good victory
**Eve** life *or* living
**Ezekiel** God strengthens
**Ezra** help

**Felix** happy

**Gabriel** man of God
**Gad** fortune
**Gamaliel** reward of God
**Gershom** alien
**Gideon** hewer

**Hagar** emigration *or* forsaken
**Ham** hot
**Hannah** grace

**Heber** associate
**Hephzibah** my delight is in her
**Hezekiah** Jehovah has strengthened
**Hiram** *possibly* my brother is exalted

**Ira** *probably* watchful
**Isaac** he laughs *or* laughter
**Ishmael** God hears
**Israel** God strives

**Jabez** he makes sorrowful
**Jacob** supplanter
**Jael** wild goat
**James** supplanter
**Japheth** God will enlarge
**Jared** *possibly* rose
**Jason** to heal
**Jehoshaphat** Jehovah is judge
**Jemima** dove
**Jephthah** opened
**Jeremiah** may Jehovah exalt
**Jesse** Jehovah exists
**Jessica** God beholds

We've decided to call him Esau.

**Jesus** Jehovah is salvation
**Jethro** excellence
**Job** afflicted *or* persecuted
**Joel** Jehovah is God
**John** Jehovah has been gracious
**Jonah** dove
**Jonathan** Jehovah has given
**Joseph** may Jehovah add
**Joshua** Jehovah is salvation
**Josiah** may Jehovah heal
**Jotham** Jehovah is perfect
**Judah** *possibly* praised
**Jude** *possibly* praised
**Judith** Jewess

**Keren** horn of antimony, i.e.
beautifier (short for Keren Happuch)
**Keturah** fragrance
**Keziah** cassia

**Laban** white
**Lazarus** God is my help
**Leah** *possibly* wild cow
**Lemuel** devoted to God
**Levi** joined
**Luke** of Lucania
**Lydia** woman of Lydia

**Magdalen** woman of Magdala
**Manasseh** one who forgets
**Marah** bitter
**Mark** *probably derived from* Mars
**Martha** lady
**Mary** wished-for child *or* rebellion
**Matthew** gift of Jehovah
**Michael** Who is like God?

**Miriam** wished-for child *or* rebellion
**Moses** son *or* drawn out

**Naomi** pleasant
**Nathan** gift
**Nathaniel** gift of God

**Paul** small
**Peter** rock
**Philip** lover of horses
**Phoebe** shining
**Priscilla** ancient

**Rachel** ewe
**Rebecca** knotted cord
**Reuben** behold a son
**Rhoda** rose
**Ruth** *perhaps* companion

**Salome** peace
**Samson** sun child
**Samuel** name of God *or* heard by
God

**Sapphire** beautiful
**Sarah** princess
**Saul** asked for
**Seth** appointed *or* granted
**Simeon** hearing
**Simon** hearing
**Solomon** peaceful
**Stephen** crown
**Susan** lily
**Susannah** lily

**Tabitha** gazelle
**Tamar** palm tree
**Thomas** twin
**Timothy** honoured by God
**Tobias** Jehovah is good

**Uriah** Jehovah is light

**Vashti** beautiful

**Zachariah** Jehovah remembers

# What's in a name?

We may refer to a traitor as a 'Judas' … or we may feel we need 'the wisdom of Solomon' … or we may describe a conversion as 'a real road-to-Damascus experience'. In this section we consider words and expressions which are derived from personal names and place names,

## PERSONAL NAMES

Two plants have been named after Aaron, the brother of Moses. '**Aaron's beard**' is another name for rose of Sharon (also called St John's wort). Its Latin name is *Hypericum calycinum*. It is a creeping shrub with large yellow flowers. The name derives from Psalm 133:2, 'It is like the precious ointment upon the head, that ran down the beard, even Aaron's beard: that went down to the skirts of his garments.'

'**Aaron's rod**' (Verbascum thapsus) is a plant that has tall spikes of yellow flowers and broad hairy leaves. In the book of Numbers (17:1–13) twelve rods (one of them Aaron's) were placed in the tabernacle. By the next day Aaron's rod had budded, blossomed and produced almonds – hence the name of the plant.

'**Abigail**' is an archaic term for a lady's maid. The name was originally that of Nabal's wife in 1 Samuel 25. Abigail apologized for her husband's meanness in refusing to give food to David's followers. She herself provided food for them, waylaying David even as he planned to attach Nabal and his people. In the space of 17 verses Abigail refers to herself as 'thine handmaid' six times. Later, after Nabal's death, Abigail became David's wife. The name came to be associated with the position of lady's maid

# Names and titles of God

## GOD

Creator (Isaiah 40:28)
Creator of heavenly lights (James 1:17)
Everlasting God (Genesis 21:33)
Father (Malachi 2:10; Matthew 6:9)
God Almighty (*El-Shaddai*) (Genesis 17:1)
God Most High (*El Elyon*) (Genesis 14:18)
God of Heaven (Nehemiah 2:4)
God of Israel (Joshua 24:2)
Heavenly Father (Matthew 6:26)
Holy God (Job 6:10)
Holy God of Israel (Isaiah 1:4)
I AM (Exodus 3:14)
Judge (Genesis 18:25)
King (Jeremiah 10:7)
King of kings (1 Timothy 6:15)
Living God (Deuteronomy 5:26)
LORD (Jehovah) (Exodus 3:13–16)
LORD Almighty (*Jehovah-Tsebahoth*, Sabaoth) (1 Samuel 1:11)
LORD is my Banner (*Jehovah-Nissi*) (Exodus 17:15)
LORD is Peace (*Jehovah-Shalom*) (Judges 6:24)
LORD of lords (1 Timothy 6:15)
LORD Our Salvation (*Jehovah Tsidkenu*) (Jeremiah 23:6)
LORD Provides (*Jehovah-Jireh*) (Genesis 22:14)
Saviour (Isaiah 44:24)
Sovereign LORD (*Adonai Yahweh*) (Genesis 15:2)

## JESUS

Bread of life (John 6:35)
Bright Morning Star (Revelation 22:16)
Christ (John 1:41)
Descendant of David (Matthew 1:1)
Eternal Father (Isaiah 9:6)
First and Last (Revelation 1:8)
Gate (John 10:7)
God's Holy Messenger (Mark 1:24)
Good Shepherd (John 10:11)
Holy and Good (Acts 3:14)
I Am (John 8:58)
Immanuel (Isaiah 7:14)
Jesus (Matthew 1:21)
King of kings (Revelation 17:14)
Lamb (Revelation 5:6–14)
Lamb of God (John 1:29)
Last Adam (1 Corinthians 15:45)
Light of the world (John 8:12)
Lion from Judah's tribe (Revelation 5:5)
Lord of lords (Revelation 17:14)
Messiah (Matthew 16:16)
Mighty God (Isaiah 9:6)
Nazarene (Matthew 2:23)
Prince of Peace (Isaiah 9:6)
Real vine (John 15:1)
Resurrection and life (John 11:25)
Saviour (Luke 2:11)
Son of God (Mark 1:1)
Son of Man (Matthew 8:20)
Way, truth and life (John 14:6)
Wonderful Counsellor (Isaiah 9:6)
Word (John 1:1)
Word of God (Revelation 19:13)

## THE HOLY SPIRIT

Eternal Spirit (Hebrews 9:14)
Helper (John 14:16)
Holy Spirit (Luke 11:13)
Power of God (Luke 1:35)
Spirit (Romans 8:26–27)
Spirit of Christ (Romans 8:9)
Spirit of his [God's] Son (Galatians 4:6)
Spirit of the Lord (Judges 3:10)
Spirit who makes us God's children (Romans 8:15)
Spirit of truth (John 14:17)

# Descriptions of the church

Believers (Acts 2:44)
Body of Christ (1 Corinthians 12:27)
Bride (Revelation 21:2)
Called (Romans 8:30;
1 Corinthians 1:2)
Chosen race (1 Peter 2:9)
Christians (Acts 11:26)
Church (Matthew 16:18; 18:17;
1 Corinthians 1:2)
Citizens of heaven
(Philippians 3:20)
Disciples (Acts 6:1)
God's building (1 Corinthians 3:9)
God's children (John 1:12;
Romans 8:14–23)
God's chosen people (1 Peter 1:1)
God's household (1 Timothy 3:15)
God's partners (1 Corinthians 3:9)

God's people in the light
(Ephesians 5:8)
God's temple (1 Corinthians 3:16)
Heirs of God (Romans 8:17)
Holy City (Revelation 21: 10–27)
Holy nation (1 Peter 2:9)
Light of the world (Matthew 5:14)
Living stones (1 Peter 2:5)
People of God (Ephesians 1:1,15,18;
3:18)
Pillar and support of the truth (1
Timothy 3:15)
Priests of the King (1 Peter 2:9)
Salt for the human race
(Matthew 5:13)
Sheep (John 10:3)
Soldiers of Christ Jesus
(2 Timothy 2:3–4)

because 'Abigail' was the name of the waiting gentlewoman' in the play, The Scornful Lady by Sir Francis Beaumont and John Fletcher, which was performed in 1610.

The phrase '**Abraham's bosom**' refers to the sleeping-place of the blessed in death. It is well known from Shakespeare's *Richard III* (Act 4, Scene 3): 'The sons of Edward sleep in Abraham's bosom.' But originally it was a figure of speech used by Jesus in the parable of Lazarus and the rich man (Luke 16:19–31): 'The beggar [Lazarus] died, and was carried by the

angels into Abraham's bosom' (verse 22).

The visible projection at the front of the neck formed by the thyroid cartilage is called the '**Adam's apple**'. It is traditionally thought that this name derives from the belief that a piece of apple from the forbidden tree became stuck in Adam's throat. It is, however, interesting to note that the Bible text nowhere mentions that the fruit was in fact an apple.

'**Adam's ale**' is water: the first human would have had nothing else to drink.

The expression 'the **old Adam**' refers to the sinful nature of all human beings.

If '**one doesn't know someone from Adam**', one doesn't recognize him or her – one has no idea who he or she is: 'I think you'd better explain to Mrs Nicholson who I am – she won't know me from Adam.' The expression derives from the fact that Adam, as the first man, is someone whom one could not know.

The word '**Ananias**', meaning a liar, alludes to the Ananias of the New Testament (Acts 5:1–10). Ananias and his wife Sapphira kept for themselves part of the money from the sale of land that was intended for the church. Ananias was struck dead after Peter declared that he had lied not to men but to God. Later Sapphira, continuing her husband's deception that they had given the full sum received to the church, in turn fell down dead.

The expression, '**to raise Cain**', meaning to 'behave in a wild, noisy manner; to cause a loud disturbance; to protest angrily' derives from the biblical Cain, the eldest son of Adam and Eve, the brother of Abel and the first murderer in the Bible (Genesis 4:3–12). It seems that in earlier times, Cain was a euphemism for the devil, religious people preferring 'raise Cain' to 'raise the devil'.

Two expressions derive from the judgement of God on Cain after he killed Abel. '**The curse of Cain**', the fate of someone who is forced to lead a fugitive life wandering restlessly from place to place, derives from the punishment mentioned in Genesis 4:11–12: 'And now art thou cursed from the earth ... a fugitive and a vagabond shalt thou be in the earth.'

'**The mark of Cain**' is a stain on one's reputation caused by a crime which one has committed. The expression refers to the protective mark which God gave Cain to prevent him from being killed himself: 'And the Lord set a mark upon Cain, lest any finding him should kill him' (Genesis 4:15).

The expression, '**a Daniel come to judgment**' refers to someone who makes a wise decision about something that has puzzled others. It alludes to the Daniel in the book of that name (5:14–16), and especially to the devout and upright young man of the apocryphal book of Susanna. The source of the actual expression is Shakespeare's *Merchant of Venice* (Act 4, Scene 1):

A Daniel comes to judgment!
yea a Daniel!

O wise young judge, how I do honour thee!

The phrase, '**Daniel in the lions' den**', referring to someone who is in a place where he or she is exposed to intense personal danger, alludes to Daniel 6.

The David in the phrase '**David and Goliath**' and '**David and Jonathan**' is the Old Testament King of Israel. The youngest son of Jesse, David was anointed by Samuel as the successor to King Saul. Goliath, as is well known, was the Philistine giant who was slain by the seemingly insignificant David. Goliath, an armoured champion, had a sword, a javelin, and a spear, while David, a mere shepherd boy, had just a staff, five smooth stones in a bag and a sling. Yet, with God's help, David slung a stone that killed the giant (1 Samuel 17). The expression, 'David and Goliath' is used, therefore, to refer to a contest between someone who is apparently weak and someone who seems to possess overwhelmingly superior strength.

David became a close friend of Jonathan, Saul's eldest son, and the Bible records their mutual loyalty and affection (1 Samuel 20). So the expression, '**David and Jonathan**' refers to close friends of the same sex.

A '**Delilah**' is a treacherous and seductive woman, especially a mistress or wife. The use of this name alludes to the story of the Old Testament character Delilah who was bribed by the Philistine rulers to discover the secret of Samson's great strength (Judges 16:4–22). Samson lied to her on three occasions, but when she continued to ask him, he grew so weary of her nagging that he told her the truth – that the source of his power lay in his long hair. Delilah then betrayed this secret to the Philistines, and while Samson slept upon her lap, his hair was shaved off. Thus he was deprived of his strength.

'**Dives**' is the name given to the rich man in the story told by Jesus in Luke 16:19–31. In the story, Dives pays no attention to the plight of Lazarus, the beggar at his gate. After death Lazarus is carried to 'Abraham's bosom' and Dives to hell, and it is not possible for there to be any contact between them. It is interesting to note that the rich man is not actually named in the English Bible text. In the Vulgate, the Latin version of the Bible, he is called '**dives**', meaning 'rich' or 'a rich man', and this word has come to be thought of as a proper noun. The name of Dives has thus become proverbial for a very rich person, especially one who is unconcerned and hard, and insensitive to others' needs.

# Christian names

In the period following 1066 English Christian names tended to be Norman-French in origin. Later, names tended to be Christian in a more literal sense, since the Church encouraged parents to use names of Christian significance. In the 16th century the split between Roman Catholics and Protestants was reflected in name usage. The Protestants turned away from Catholic names such as **Mary**, and from the names of saints such as **Augustine** and **Benedict, Barbara** and **Agnes**. They preferred to use the Bible as their principal source of names, especially the Old Testament. It was then that Hebrew names such as **Aaron, Abraham, Adam, Benjamin, Daniel, David, Jacob, Jonathan, Joseph, Joshua, Michael, Nathan, Noah, Samuel, Saul, Seth,** and **Solomon** were brought into use for boys, while the girls became **Abigail, Beulah, Deborah, Dinah, Esther, Eve, Hannah, Keziah, Leah, Miriam, Naomi, Rachel, Rebekah, Ruth, Sarah,** and **Tamar**. These names were later to become especially associated with the USA, since religious persecution would force the Protestant groups to emigrate.

Not all the Old Testament names, incidentally, were as familiar and pleasant as those mentioned above. At this time children also received names such as **Amaziah, Belteshazzar, Habakkuk, Jehoshaphat,**

**Nebuchadnezzar**, and **Onesiphorous** (boys); **Aholibamah, Eglah, Abishag**, and **Maachah** (girls).

It was in the 16th and 17th centuries that the religious extremists known as Puritans appeared on the scene. For some of them, even the names that had biblical sanction were not pure enough. They gave their children slogan names, such as **Be-courteous, Faint-not, Fight-the-good-fight-of-faith, Fly-fornication, Make-peace, Safe-deliverance, Stand-fast-on-high, The Lord-is-near**. Such names were much laughed at by the general public, of course, and eventually sanity reasserted itself.

MY NAME IS 'DESTRUCTION-VISITETH-THE-UNRIGHTEOUS'. CALL ME 'DES' FOR SHORT.

The more sensible Puritans had in the meantime managed to display their religious beliefs in less eccentric ways, creating a group of names which have survived to the present day, including **Amity, Charity, Faith, Felicity, Grace, Honour, Hope, Joy, Mercy, Patience, Prudence** and **Verity**.

A **Dorcas society** is a Christian charitable society of women who meet to make clothes for the poor. The name derives from Dorcas (or Tabitha), a Christian disciple in Joppa who was well known for her works of charity. When she died, her friends sent for Peter. Peter prayed, and she was raised from the dead. Her resurrection led many to faith (Acts 9:36–43).

**The Gideons** are an interdenominational Christian group who have the aim of making the Bible freely available. Originally founded by three Christian commercial travellers – Samuel E Hill, William J Knights and John H Nicholson – in Wisconsin, USA, in 1899, the organization places Bibles in hotel rooms, hospital wards, prisons, etc. It is named after Gideon, the Old Testament judge famous for leading the small army which triumphed over the Midianites (Judges 6–7).

It was through an unexpected event that the Gideons came into being. John Nicholson 'just happened' to be sharing a hotel bedroom with Samuel Hill in September 1898. Before going to sleep, Nicholson read a portion of the Bible – he had promised his dying mother at the age of 13 that he would read the Bible every day. So it was through Nicholson's faithfulness in reading the Bible that the two room-mates discovered that they were both Christians … and so the idea of a Christian fellowship for commercial travellers was born.

In 1903 a Gideon from Chicago who was visiting England discovered that the Christian Association for Commercial Travellers – which had been in existence for some 30 years – was placing Bibles in hotels. He took the idea back with him to America, and in 1908 the Gideons started putting Bibles in hotels in the USA.

The expression, '**to out-herod Herod**' means 'to exceed someone in a particular quality, especially wickedness or cruelty'. The Herod referred to is Herod the Great (*c.* 73–74 BC), the ruler of Judaea who had all the baby boys of Bethlehem killed (Matthew 2:16). The source of the expression itself is Shakespeare's *Hamlet* (Act 3, Scene 2): 'I would have such a fellow shipped for o'erdoing Termagant; it out-herods Herod: pray you, avoid it.'

An '**Ishmael**' is a social outcast. The expression comes from the Bible character Ishmael, the son of Abraham and Hagar, the Egyptian maidservant of Sarah. According to the biblical narrative (Genesis 16–25), when Sarah realized that she could not conceive children, she gave her maidservant to Abraham so that she might conceive by proxy. When Hagar became pregnant, she began to despise her mistress, who then drove her out of her home. An angel of Jehovah met Hagar and told her to return and submit to Sarah, saying that her descendants through Ishmael would be innumerable – God also assured Abraham that Ishmael would be the father of twelve rulers and ultimately of a great nation. When in due course Sarah bore a son, Isaac, by Abraham, she insisted that Ishmael and Hagar be expelled from the home. In the desert, the outcasts nearly perished for lack of water, but God provided them with a well of water. Ishmael grew up to become an archer, and Hagar found a wife for him. He did indeed become the father of twelve sons.

Ishmael is the name of the narrator in Herman Melville's *Moby Dick* (1851), which opens with the striking line, 'Call me Ishmael.'

'**Jacob's ladder**' is the name given to two things – a ladder used on board ship and a plant. The former of the two is made of rope or cable and has wooden or metal rungs. It is dropped over the side of a ship to allow people to ascend from or descend to small boats positioned alongside. The plant known as Jacob's ladder (*Polemonium caeruleum*) has blue or white flowers and light green leaves which grow in a ladder-like arrangement.

The origin of the phrase, '**Jacob's ladder**' is to be found in Genesis 28:12. It was the ladder resting on the earth and reaching to heaven, that Jacob, father of the twelve tribes of Israel, saw in a dream.

A **Jehovah's Witness** is a member of the religious movement originally founded in 1872 by Charles Taze Russell (1852–1916). Members of the organization aim to follow the literal sense of the Christian Bible, but they reject some basic tenets of established Christianity, especially the doctrine of the Trinity and the deity of Jesus Christ and the Holy Spirit. Jehovah's Witnesses are known for their zealous door-to-door personal evangelism.

Jehovah's Witnesses use the personal name *Jehovah* for God – the name which he revealed to Moses on Mount Horeb (Exodus 3:13–15). The word *Jehovah* (also *Yahweh*) comes from Hebrew *YHVH*, known as the 'tetragrammaton'. Because this name was regarded as too sacred to be pronounced, it was replaced by the word *Adonai* ('my Lord') when the Scriptures were read. The vowel sounds *a*, *o*, and *a* from *Adonai* were inserted into the word *YHVH*, hence *YaHoVaH* and *Jehovah*. The form *Jehovah* is first attested at the beginning of twelfth century AD.

# King-size bottles

A '**jeroboam**' (also known as a 'double magnum') is a very large wine bottle. It holds the equivalent of four standard wine bottles, a standard bottle having a capacity of 0.7 litre or 0.75 litre. It seems that the name was first humorously given to such bottles in the 19th century, the allusion being to Jeroboam, the first king of the northern kingdom of Israel. The biblical text describes him as 'a mighty man of valour' (1 Kings 11:28) and says that he 'did sin, and … made Israel to sin' (1 Kings 14:16). The bottle is without doubt 'mighty' and the alcoholic drink contained in it could certainly lead to sin!

Other bottle sizes named after Old Testament figures include:

- The '**rehoboam**', six standard wine bottles – named after Rehoboam, a son of Solomon, the last king of the united Israel and the first king of Judah. His name means 'expansion of the people'
- The '**methuselah**', eight standard wine bottles – after the patriarch Methuselah, who lived to 969 years (Genesis 5:27).
- The '**salmanazar**', twelve standard wine bottles – after Shalmaneser, king of Assyria (2 Kings 17:3).
- The '**balthazar**', 16 standard wine bottles – after King Belshazzar of Babylon, who drank wine at the great feast (Daniel 5:1).
- The '**nebuchadnezzar**', 20 standard wine bottles – after King Nebuchadnezzar of Babylon.

Another nebuchadnezzar of wine, sir?

The Hebrew word *Yahweh* or *Jehovah* is usually translated as 'the LORD' in English versions of the Bible.

A '**jeremiad**' is a lengthy lamentation or complaint. The word comes via French from the name of Jeremiah, the Old Testament prophet. The biblical book of Jeremiah contains many prophecies of judgment, particularly against idolatry, immorality, and false prophets, and so Jeremiah is sometimes known as the Prophet of Doom. Thus the word '**Jeremiah**' has come to be used to refer to a pessimistic person who foresees a gloomy future or one who condemns the society he lives in.

A **Jesuit** is a member of the Society of Jesus, the Roman Catholic religious order founded by St Ignatius Loyola in 1534. Its original aims were to defend Catholicism against the Reformation and to undertake missionary work in the unbelieving world. The word 'Jesuit' comes from Late Latin *Jesus* (Jesus Christ), the suffix *-ita* meaning 'follower' or 'supporter'.

Because of a tendency of a few Jesuits, especially in the 17th century, to be concerned with politics, the word 'Jesuit' and the adjective 'Jesuitical' are sometimes used to refer to a person who is involved in subtle intrigue or cunning deception.

'**Jethroization**' is the principle of delegating responsibility and authority to others. The term derives from the advice of Jethro to his son-in-law Moses in Exodus 18:1–27. Moses was judging cases all day long and Jethro could see that the strain was wearing Moses out. Jethro proposed that Moses should continue to be God's representative. He should teach the people laws, but should delegate responsibility for deciding simple cases to capable men, who would officiate over thousands, hundreds, fifties, and tens of people. Only difficult cases would be brought to Moses.

A '**Jezebel**' is a shameless, scheming or immoral woman. The word comes from the biblical Jezebel, daughter of Ethbaal, king of Tyre and Sidon, who married Ahab, the king of Israel. Jezebel's notorious wickedness is described in 1 and 2 Kings. She worshipped the fertility god Baal and persuaded Ahab and his people to follow her religion. Under her orders, God's prophets were killed, and were replaced by the prophets of Baal. In answer to Elijah's prayer, God defeated Baal at Mount Carmel. Jezebel then resolved to kill Elijah, who was forced to go into hiding. After the incident over Naboth's vineyard, Elijah predicted Jezebel's violent end, and some time later she was thrown down from a high palace window.

The Old Testament figure of Job was a man of upright character who lost his wealth, his ten children, and his health. Satan brought these disasters on him, with God's permission. The book of Job tells how he kept his faith in God in the midst of all his afflictions. Thus to have '**the patience of Job**' means to endure difficulties, misfortunes or laborious tasks with supreme patience, courage and tolerance.

Job was visited by three friends who gave him the advice of popular opinion, emphasizing particularly that his misfortunes were brought about by his own disobedience to God. From these friends, whom Job refers to as 'miserable comforters' (Job 16:2) comes the expression, **'a Job's comforter'** used to describe someone whose attempts to bring encouragement result in discouragement and distress.

A **'Jonah'** is a person who is believed to bring bad luck. The expression derives from the biblical Jonah, the Hebrew prophet who was held responsible for the storm that struck the ship he was travelling in (Jonah 1:4–7). Jonah had run away from God and had boarded the ship, which was bound for Tarshish, disobeying God's command to go to Nineveh to denounce its people.

A **'jorum'** is a large drinking bowl, named after Joram, son of King Toi of Hamath. Joram brought to King David 'vessels of silver, and vessels of gold, and vessels of brass' to congratulate him on his victory in battle over Hadadezer (2 Samuel 8:9–10).

A **'Judas'** is a traitor, a person who betrays a friend. The word comes from the name of Christ's betrayer, Judas Iscariot.

The name Judas occurs in a number of expressions that allude to betrayal or cunning. A **'Judas kiss'** is a show of affection that conceals treachery. A **'Judas slit'** is a peep-hole in a door through which guards can observe their prisoners. A **'Judas tree'** is an ornamental shrub or tree of the genus *Cercis*. Its pinkish-purple flowers bloom before the leaves appear. The genus is so called because it is traditionally thought that Judas hanged himself on such a tree.

A **'lazaret'** or **'lazaretto'** is a hospital for people with contagious diseases, or a building or ship used for quarantine, or a ship's storeroom. The words are derived from a combination of the words *lazar* and *Nazaret*. *Lazar* is an archaic word for a poor, diseased person, especially a leper, and comes from *Lazarus*, the name of the beggar in Jesus' parable (Luke 16:20). *Nazaret* is short for *Santa Maria di Nazaret*, a church in Venice that maintained a hospital.

The word **'magdalen'** (or **'magdalene'**) means 'a reformed prostitute' or 'a house of refuge or of reform for prostitutes'. It comes from the name of Mary Magdalene, a woman healed by Jesus of evil spirits (Luke 8:2) and the first person to whom the risen Jesus appeared (John 20:1–18). Traditionally Mary

Magdalen is often identified with the sinful woman of Luke 7:36–50, and considered to have been a reformed prostitute, though the biblical text does not justify such a conclusion.

A '**Martha**' is a woman who is busily occupied wlth domestic matters (especially preparing meals), in contrast to a '**Mary**', a woman who leads a quieter, more contemplative life. These names belonged to two sisters who were friends of Jesus. On one occasion at Martha's home (Luke 10:38–42) Mary sat at Jesus' feet listening to his words, while Martha was actively bustling away, preparing a meal. Martha's complaint about Mary's inactivity met with a gentle rebuke from Jesus.

The expression, '**as old as Methuselah**', meaning 'very old', refers to the age of the Old Testament patriarch of that name. According to Genesis 5, Methuselah was the son of Enoch and the grandfather of Noah, and lived to be 969 years old.

A portable, shallow, wickerwork cradle for a baby is sometimes known as a '**Moses basket**'. This expression alludes to the papyrus cradle into which the infant Moses was placed, among the reeds by the River Nile (Exodus 2:3).

A '**Naboth's vineyard**' is a possession greatly coveted by someone who has no scruples about obtaining it for himself or herself. The allusion is to the story related in 1 Kings 21. A vineyard belonging to Naboth the Jezreelite lay close to King Ahab's palace. Ahab coveted the vineyard, but Naboth refused to sell it. So Ahab's wife Jezebel undertook to obtain it for him by having Naboth falsely accused of blasphemy and then stoned to death. when Ahab went to take possession of the vineyard, the prophet Elijah met him and pronounced judgment on him and his descendants.

If someone is called a '**Nimrod**' it means that he is a great, skilful hunter. The allusion is to the biblical Nimrod,

# Now Barabbas was a publisher

This expression is often attributed to the English poet Lord Byron (1788–1824). Byron, it is said, received a copy of a splendid edition of the Bible from the publisher John Murray as an expression of thanks for a favour. Byron, so the story goes, returned the copy, having substituted the word *publisher* for *robber* in the text of John 18:40, 'Now Barabbas was a robber.'

the son of Cush, who was a warrior or hero of Babylon. Genesis 10:9 describes him as 'a mighty hunter before the Lord'. Nimrod is credited with the founding of the cities of Nineveh and Calah (modern Nimrud) in Assyria (Genesis 10:11).

The term, '**onanism**' refers to two sexual practices: coitus interruptus and masturbation. The word derives from the name of the biblical character Onan, who 'spilled it [his semen] on the ground' (Genesis 38:9), although it seems that the biblical passage describes coitus interruptus rather than masturbation. When Onan's elder brother, Er, died, Judah commanded Onan to take his brother's wife Tamar, since the levirate law stipulated that if a married man died without a child, his brother should take his wife. Onan, however, was not willing to follow this practice and did not fully consummate the union, and so the Lord put him to death.

A '**Rechabite**' is a total abstainer from alcoholic drink, particularly a member of the Independent Order of Rechabites, a society founded in 1835 and devoted to total abstention from alcohol. The biblical Rechabites or descendants of Rechab (Recab) drank no wine, since their ancestor had commanded it (Jeremiah 35:1–19).

Jeremiah used the example of the Rechabites' obedience to their forefather as a way of sharply rebuking the people of Judah and Jerusalem for their lack of obedience to God.

A man of great strength is sometimes known as a '**Samson**'. The allusion here is to the judge of Israel of that name. Samson's outstanding feats of strength included tearing a lion apart with his bare hands, catching 300 foxes and then tying them tail to tail in pairs, and striking down 1,000 men with the jawbone of a donkey.

When the treacherous Delilah eventually discovered that the secret of his strength lay in his hair, she had it all shaved off so that his strength left him. The Philistines seized him and gouged out his eyes.

Samson's final act was to entertain the Philistines at the temple of

Dagon. His hair had by now grown again, and so, calling upon God, he braced himself against the two central pillars that supported the temple. Above him were about 3,000 people. He pushed with all his strength, so destroying the temple. Thus he killed himself and more Philistines than he had killed during his whole life.

The term '**simony**' means the practice of buying or selling church or spiritual benefits or offices, and alludes to Simon Magus, a sorcerer mentioned in the book of Acts. After becoming a Christian, Simon tried to buy the gift of spiritual power from the Apostles, but was strongly rebuked by Peter (Acts 8:9–24).

Solomon was a tenth-century BC King of Israel and was the son of King David and Bathsheba. He was noted for his great wisdom and wealth. His wisdom has become proverbial, and is alluded to in expressions such as '**one needs the wisdom of Solomon**' and '**as wise as Solomon**'. This wisdom was demonstrated when two women came to him, each claiming that a particular baby was her own. Solomon's suggestion that the baby be divided in two revealed the true mother – she was the woman who would rather let her rival have the baby than see him killed (1 Kings 3:16–28).

'**Solomon's seal**' is the name given to lilies of the genus *Polygonatum*. They have greenish-white flowers, long smooth leaves, and a fleshy white underground stem. The stem is marked with prominent leaf scars, which are said to resemble seals – hence the name. 'Solomon's seal' is also another name for the Star of David, a mystic symbol traditionally associated with Solomon.

A '**doubting Thomas**' is someone who is sceptical, particularly someone who refuses to believe until he or she has seen proof of something or has been otherwise satisfied as to its truth. The expression alludes to Thomas, one of Jesus' apostles, who refused to believe in Christ's resurrection until he had seen and felt Christ's body for himself (John 20:24–29).

## PLACE NAMES
An '**adullamite**' is a person who has withdrawn from a political party to join a new dissident group. The term was originally applied to rebels in the British House of Commons who withdrew from the Liberal party in 1866. The allusion is to the cave of Adullam, to which David and others fled when pursued by Saul (1 Samuel 22:1–2). The city of Adullam lay midway between Jerusalem and Lachish, south-west of Bethlehem.

The name '**Armageddon**' is sometimes given to a vast and extremely destructive conflict, particularly the final war between good and evil at the end of the world. The word is mentioned only in Revelation 16:16, as the meeting-place in the apocalyptic scene of the great day of God Almighty. The word 'Armageddon' probably means 'mountain of Megiddo'. Megiddo is a place about 20 miles south-west of Nazareth; in the past many decisive battles have been fought near it.

A '**babel**' in modern English is a confusion of sounds or voices or a noisy or chaotic scene. The expression comes from the biblical tower of Babel, built with the intention of reaching to heaven (Genesis 11:1–9). God confounded the builders' efforts by causing them to speak different languages so that they could not understand one another.

To have a '**Damascus experience**' is to have a sudden conversion in one's beliefs. Hence someone's conversion is sometimes referred to as his or her '**road to Damascus**'. The expressions allude to the experience of Saul of Tarsus, who, while on his way to the city of Damascus to persecute Christianity there, encountered Jesus Christ. Suddenly a light shone around him (hence our phrase '**see the light**'); he fell to the ground, and he heard Christ speak to him (Acts 9:1–9). So he became Christ's disciple and apostle.

## The Dominion of Canada

The delegates of the British North American colonies at the Confederation conferences (1864, 66–67) originally wanted to refer to the new nation of Canada as the Kingdom of Canada. The British government, however, fearing the sensitivity of Americans to references to the Crown and anxious not to antagonize them after the US Civil War, insisted that another title be found. The Canadian politician Sir Leonard Tilley (1818–96) suggested the term, 'dominion', from Psalm 72:8, 'He shall have dominion also from sea to sea' (AV). The title was intended to give dignity to the federation and to be tribute to the monarchical principle. Under the Constitution Act, 1982, 'Dominion' remains Canada's official title.

The expression, '**from Dan to Beersheba**' is sometimes used to mean 'from one end of the country to another'. The phrase refers to the most northerly city (Dan) and most southerly town (Beersheba) of Palestine (Judges 20:1).

The adjective, **'Gadarene'** is sometimes used to mean 'engaged in a headlong rush'. The word refers to the 'country of the Gergesenes' (Matthew 8:28), where Jesus cast the demons out of two possessed men into a herd of swine. The demons caused the pigs to rush down a steep slope into the sea of Galilee, where they drowned. The site of the miracle was at the eastern edge of the sea, in a sub-district of the capital Gadara, which lay to the south-east.

The city of **Jericho** was regarded as a formidable obstacle by the Israelites. After the two spies had searched it (Joshua 2), Joshua led his forces against the city, marching around it daily for six days. On the seventh day they circled it seven times, then shouted and blew their trumpets. The wall collapsed; every man charged straight in, and they took the city (Joshua 6). The miraculous fall of the walls of Jericho is sometimes alluded to in descriptions of sudden victories gained without striking a blow.

The expression, **'the new Jerusalem'** is used to mean heaven, paradise or a perfect community. The phrase derives from Revelation 21:2, 'And I John saw the holy city, new Jerusalem, coming down from God out of heaven, prepared as a bride adorned for her husband. The expression, **'pearly gates'**, meaning the entrance to heaven, alludes to Revelation 21:21.

The term, **'Laodicean'** is used to describe someone who is lukewarm and indifferent, especially in religious or political matters. The origin of this term is the criticism expressed by Christ of the church at Laodicea (Revelation 3:14–22). The believers there were neither cold nor hot, but showed a tepid, half-hearted commitment.

To be in **'the land of Nod'** (or **'nod'**) is to be asleep. The phrase derives from Genesis 4:16, which refers to the region to which Cain was banished after he had killed Abel: 'And Cain went out from the presence of the Lord and dwelt in the land of Nod, on the east of Eden.' The Hebrew name means 'wandering'. The expression, 'the land of Nod', suggesting the nodding of a drowsy head, is probably a pun.

**Sodom and Gomorrah** (two of the 'cities of the plain') were cities that were notorious for vice and depravity and were destroyed by God (Genesis 18:16–19:29). The cities are repeatedly mentioned in the Bible with reference to God's judgment (see e.g. Isaiah 1:9–10; Amos 4:11; Luke 17:29; 2 Peter 2:6; Jude 7). **Sodomy** is anal intercourse between a man and another man or a woman; the word alludes to the homosexual desire of the men of Sodom (Genesis 19:1–11).

# Bible numbers

Some biblical numbers have a symbolic or theological significance.

**1:** unity, especially of God (Deuteronomy 6:4; John 17:21; Acts 17:26; Romans 5:12,15).

**2:** unity (Genesis 1:27; 2:24); division; separateness (1 Kings 18:21; Matthew 25:31–46).

---

## 666 – The number of the beast

(See Revelation 13:18.) 'What does the number of the beast mean? Any amount of ink has been spilt over this fascinating, and misleading, question. The number is said to stand for Nero, or Caligula, or Domitian, or the Caesars in general, or the Roman Empire, or any one of several solutions, mostly based on the fact that in Greek and Hebrew as well as in Latin, numerals were indicated by letters of the alphabet, so that the letters of various names had numerical values which could be added together to obtain the total 666. More recent candidates have included Mohammed, Cromwell, and Napoleon, not to mention Martin Luther and an assortment of popes. The number has also been used to calculate possible dates when the beast might appear. For example, *qsr nron* (a Hebrew spelling of 'Caesar Nero') adds up to this: 100 + 6 + 200 and 50 + 200 + 6 + 50.

'It is our contention that all such answers are wrong, because the question itself is wrong. The number does not stand for any particular person or institution. The number simply stands for *the beast*. (Michael Wilcock, *The Message of Revelation: I saw heaven opened*, Inter-Varsity Press.)

'Six, moreover, is not seven and never reaches seven. It ever fails to attain to perfection; that is, it never becomes seven. Six means missing the mark, failure. Seven means perfection, victory. Rejoice, O church of God! The victory is on thy side. The number of the beast is 666, that is, failure upon failure upon failure! It is the number of MAN, for the beast glories in Man; hence must fail!'

William Hendriksen, *More than Conquerors*, Baker

**3:** the Trinity of persons in the Godhead; completeness (Matthew 28:19; John 14:26; 15:26); the power of God (1 Corinthians 15:4).

**4:** completion; creation; the world (Jeremiah 49:36; Revelation 7:1); the 4 Gospels.

**6:** human beings (Genesis 1:27–31 Exodus 20:9; Luke 13:14).

**7:** completion, fulfilment and perfection (Genesis 2:2; Exodus 20:10; Leviticus 16:29–30; Revelation 1:12).

**10:** completeness; the 10 commandments (Exodus 20:1–17: Daniel 7:7, 20, 24).

**12:** the people of God; the 12 tribes of Israel (Genesis 49:28); the 12 apostles (Matthew 10:1–4).

**40:** development of history and salvation; testing (Genesis 7:17; Exodus 24:18; 1 Kings 19:8; Matthew 4:2; Acts 1:3).

**70:** God's administration of the world (Genesis 10; Numbers 11:16; Daniel 9:24; Luke 10:1).

# 70 – an administrative number

The number 70 is often associated with God's administration of the world.

- After the Flood, the world was populated again through 70 descendants of Noah (Genesis 10)
- 70 (or 75) people went to Egypt (Genesis 46:27)
- 70 elders were appointed to help Moses administrate Israel (Exodus 24:1; Numbers 11:16)
- The people of Israel spent a period of 70 years in exile in Babylon (Jeremiah 25:11; 29:10)
- 70 'sevens' were decreed by God as the period in which the Messianic redemption was to be accomplished (Daniel 9:24)
- Jesus sent out 70 (or 72) disciples (Luke 10:1)
- Jesus instructed forgiveness '70 times 7' (Matthew 18:22)

# 153 – A wonderful number?

In his book, *Biblical Numerology* (Baker), John J Davis comments: 'One … text which has caught the imagination of commentators is John 21:11. Many have felt that since the exact number of fishes is given in the text, it must bear some special significance.'

St Jerome makes reference to a zoologist subsequent to John (whom, however, we now know, he misread) according to whom there are 153 species of fish. Thus the purpose of the text is to declare that in the church (= the net), without losing its unity, there is room for all the races of mankind (J.J. von Allmen).

Augustine proposed a similar view based on the fact that the sum of the factor of 17 equalled 153. His conclusion was that 'All, therefore, who are sharers in such grace are symbolized by this number, that is, are symbolically represented.'

# My friend, the Bible

## Quotations about the Bible

'The devil is not afraid of the Bible that has dust on it.'
**Anonymous**

'Read your Bible. Free gift inside!'
**Anonymous**

'Suppose a nation in some distant region should take the Bible for their only lawbook, and every member should regulate his conduct by the precepts there exhibited! ... What a Utopia; what a Paradise would this region be!'
**John Quincy Adams, US president (1767–1848)**

'In the Old Testament the new lies hidden, in the New Testament the old is laid open.'
**Saint Augustine, Bishop of Hippo, theologian and Church Father (354–430)**

'The Bible is a volume of letters from the heavenly country.'
**Saint Augustine of Hippo**

'We must be on guard against giving interpretations of scripture that are far-fetched or opposed to science, and so exposing the word of God to the ridicule of unbelievers.'
**Saint Augustine of Hippo**

'The Bible is God's chart for you to steer by, to keep you from the bottom of the sea, and to show you where the harbour is, and how to reach it without running on rocks and bars.'
**Henry Ward Beecher, US preacher and journalist (1813–87)**

'Your word is a lamp to guide me and a light for my path.'
**Psalm 119:105**

'I have hidden your word in my heart that I might not sin against you.'
**Psalm 119:11**

'I delight in your decrees; I will not neglect your word.'
**Psalm 119:16**

'The Bible is like a telescope. If a man looks through his telescope, then he sees worlds beyond; but if he looks at his telescope, then he does not see anything but that. The Bible is a thing to be looked through, to see that which is beyond; but most people only look at it; and so they see only the dead letter.'
**Phillips Brooks, US preacher and bishop (1835–93)**

'The Bible was never intended to be a book for scholars and specialists only. From the very beginning it was intended to be everybody's book, and that is what it continues to be.'
**F.F. Bruce, Scottish Bible theologian and author (1910–90)**

'... read the Bible as though it were something entirely unfamiliar, as though it had not been set before you ready-made ... Face the book with a new attitude as something new ... Let whatever may happen occur between yourself and it. You do not know which of its sayings and images will overwhelm and mould you ... But hold yourself open. Do not believe anything a priori; do not disbelieve anything a priori. Read aloud the words written in the book in front of you; hear the word you utter and let it reach you.'
**Martin Buber, Jewish philosopher and theologian (1878–1965)**

'On her deathbed, Gertrude Stein is said to have asked, "What is the answer?" Then, after a long silence,

## The bishop's car

Dr Handley Moule, Bishop of Durham 1901–20, was amongst the first ministers to own a car. The automobile's number (licence) plate was J1011. The Bishop took this to stand for John 10:11, 'I am the good shepherd: the good shepherd giveth his life for the sheep' (AV).

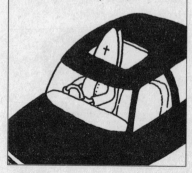

"What is the question?" Don't start looking in the Bible for the answers it gives. Start by listening for the questions it asks.'
**Frederick Buechner, US writer and minister**

'I have sometimes seen more in a line of the Bible than I could well tell how to stand under, and yet at another time the whole Bible hath been to me as dry as a stick.'
**John Bunyan, English non-Conformist minister and author (1628–88)**

'Scripture is like a pair of spectacles which dispels the darkness and gives us a clear view of God.'
**John Calvin, French-born theologian (1509–64)**

'Time can take nothing from the Bible. It is the living monitor. Like the sun, it is the same in its light and influence to man this day which it was years ago. It can meet every present inquiry and console every present loss.'
**Richard Cecil, Anglican preacher (1748–1810)**

'The Bible resembles an extensive garden, where there is a vast variety and profusion of fruits and flowers, some of which are more essential or more splendid than others; but there is not a blade suffered to grow in it which has not its use and beauty in the system.'
**Richard Cecil**

'I have worked over the Bible, prayed over the Bible for more than sixty years, and I tell you there is no book like the Bible. It is a miracle of

---

# Oh, how I love your law

How I love your law!
I think about it all day long.
Your commandment is with me all the time and makes me wiser than my enemies.
I understand more than all my teachers, because I meditate on your instructions.
I have greater wisdom than those who are old, because I obey your commands.
I have avoided all evil conduct, because I want to obey your word.
I have not neglected your instructions, for you yourself are my teacher.
How sweet is the taste of your instructions – sweeter even than honey!
I gain wisdom from your laws, and so I hate all bad conduct.
**Psalm 119:97–104 (GNB)**

literature, a perennial spring of wisdom, a wonderful book of surprises, a revelation of mystery, an infallible guide of conduct, an unspeakable source of comfort.'
**Samuel Chadwick, English evangelist (1860–1932)**

'Beware of reasoning about God's Word – obey it!'
**Oswald Chambers, Scottish evangelist, teacher and writer (1874–1917)**

'We believe that the most scientific view, the most up-to-date and rationalistic conception, will find its fullest satisfaction in taking the Bible story literally.'
**Winston Churchill, British prime minister (1874–1965)**

'Explain the Scriptures by the Scriptures.'
**St Clement of Alexandria, Greek theologian (*c.* 150–*c.* 215)**

'For more than a thousand years the Bible, collectively taken, has gone hand in hand with civilization, science, law – in short, with the moral and intellectual cultivation of the species, always supporting and often leading the way.'
**Samuel Taylor Coleridge, English poet and literary critic (1772–1834)**

'I have found in the Bible words for my inmost thoughts, songs for my joy, utterance for my hidden griefs and pleadings for my shame and feebleness.'
**Samuel Taylor Coleridge**

'The family Bible is more often used to adorn coffee tables or press flowers than it is to feed souls and discipline lives.'
**Charles Colson, US politician, founder of the Prison Fellowship (1931– )**

'After more than sixty years of almost daily reading of the Bible, I never fail to find it always new and marvelously in tune with the changing needs of every day.'
**Cecil B. DeMille, US motion picture producer and director (1881–1959)**

> **'Nobody ever outgrows Scripture; the book widens and deepens with our years.'**
> Charles Haddon Spurgeon, Baptist preacher (1834–92)

'The New Testament is the best book the world has ever known or will know.'
**Charles Dickens, English novelist (1812–70)**

'Of all commentaries upon the Scriptures, good examples are the best and liveliest.'
**John Donne, English Anglican poet and preacher (1573–1631)**

'There are two things we must never forget. In the first place, our belief in an errorless Bible is not based upon the fact that it can all be proved to be true; on the contrary we believe it because of its own claim ... The second fact that we must not forget is that as scholars discover more and more about Bible language and Bible archaeology almost all their information shows the Bible to be accurate.'
**Brian Edwards, 20th-century author**

# How to handle the Bible

1. Get *everything* out of it
2. Do not read *anything* into it
3. Let *nothing* remain unread in it.

**J.A. Bengel, Lutheran New Testament scholar (1687–1752)**

'Those who talk of the Bible as a "monument of English prose" are merely admiring it as a monument over the grave of Christianity.'
**T.S. Eliot, American-born English poet, critic and dramatist (1888–1965)**

'The Bible is my church. It is always open, and there is my High Priest ever waiting to receive me. There I have my confessional, my thanksgiving, my psalm of praise ... and a congregation of whom the world is not worthy – prophets and apostles, and martyrs and confessors – in short, all I can want, there I find.'
**Charlotte Elliott, English hymn writer (1789–1871)**

'In my own life and throughout my career in public service, I have found in the pages of the Bible a steady compass and a source of great strength and peace. As each of my predecessors in the Presidency has done, I asked for God's guidance as I undertook the duties of this office. I have asked for that guidance many times since.'
**Gerald R. Ford, US president (1913–   )**

'The word of God is in the Bible as the soul is in the body.'
**Peter Taylor Forsyth, English theologian (1848–1921)**

# How to make the best use of the Bible

1. Read it *through*
2. Pray it *in*
3. Work it *out*
4. Note it *down*
5. Pass it *on*

'The Bible grows more beautiful, as we grow in our understanding of it.'
**J.W. Goethe, German poet and dramatist (1749–1832)**

'I'm going to heaven and I believe I'm going by the blood of Christ. That's not popular preaching, but I'll tell you it's all the way through the Bible and I may be the last fellow on earth who

# Places distant from Jerusalem

The Sovereign LORD said, 'Look at Jerusalem. I put her at the centre of the world, with other countries all round her' (Ezekiel 5:5).

|  | approx. miles | km |
|---|---|---|
| Antioch | 300 | 480 |
| Ararat, Mount | 760 | 1,225 |
| Athens | 780 | 1,255 |
| Babylon | 500 | 800 |
| Beeroth | 10 | 16 |
| Beersheba | 41 | 77 |
| Bethany | 2 | 3 |
| Bethel | 12 | 19 |
| Bethlehem | 6 | 9 |
| Bethphage | 2½ | 4 |
| Cana in Galilee | 70 | 110 |
| Capernaum | 80 | 129 |
| Carmel | 75 | 120 |
| Cesarea | 70 | 110 |
| Cesarea Philippi (Paneas) | 120 | 195 |

| Chorazin | 82 | 133 |
|---|---|---|
| Corinth | 830 | 1,335 |
| Cyrene | 790 | 1,271 |
| Damascus | 136 | 219 |
| Elat | 194 | 312 |
| Emmaus (?) | 7½ | 11 |
| Gaza | 57 | 92 |
| Gethsemane | ½ | ¾ |
| Gibeon | 6 | 9 |
| Hebron | 20 | 32 |
| Jacob's Well | 33 | 53 |
| Jericho | 25 | 40 |
| Joppa | 40 | 64 |
| London (direct line) | 2,240 | 3,605 |
| Nazareth | 60 | 96 |
| New York | 6,200 | 9,978 |
| Nineveh | 570 | 917 |
| Rome | 1,450 | 2,334 |
| Samaria | 40 | 64 |
| Sychar | 34 | 55 |
| Tel Aviv | 39 | 62 |
| Tiberias | 70 | 110 |
| Tomb of Rachel | 4 | 6 |
| Tyre | 110 | 177 |

preaches it, but I'm going to preach it because it's the only way we're going to get there.'
**Billy Graham, US evangelist (1918– )**

'The Bible is the only thing that can combat the devil. Quote Scriptures and the devil will run ... use the Scriptures like a sword and you'll drive temptation away.'
**Billy Graham**

'Hold fast to the Bible as the sheet-anchor of our liberties; write its precepts on your hearts and practise them in your lives. To the influence of this book we are indebted for the progress made in true civilization, and to this we must look for our guide to the future.'
**Ulysses S. Grant, US president (1822–85)**

'It is impossible mentally or socially to enslave a Bible-reading people.'
**Horace Greeley, US politician and journalist (1811–72)**

'Holy Scripture is a stream of running water, where alike the elephant may swim, and the lamb walk without losing its feet.'
**Gregory I, Pope and saint (540–604)**

# My Bible and I

We've traveled together
  My Bible and I.
Through all kinds of weather
  With smile or with sigh.
In sorrow or sunshine,
  In tempest or calm –
Its friendship unchanging,
  My lamp and my psalm.

We've traveled together
  My Bible and I.
When life had grown weary,
  And death e'en was night.
But all through the darkness
  Of mist or of wrong,
I found there a solace,
  A prayer, and a song.

So now who shall part us,
  My Bible and I?
Shall 'isms' or 'schisms,'
  Or 'new lights' who try?
Shall shadow for substance
  Or stone for good bread,
Supplant thy sound wisdom,
  Give folly instead?

Ah, no, my dear Bible,
  Exponent of light!
Thou sword of the Spirit,
  Put error to flight!
And all through life's journey
  Until my last sigh,
We'll travel together –
  My Bible and I.

**Charles Sandford**

'The highest earthly enjoyments are but a shadow of the joy I find in reading God's word.'
**Lady Jane Grey, queen of England July 9–19, 1553 (1537–54)**

'Compare Scripture with Scripture. False doctrines, like false witnesses, agree not among themselves.'
**William Gurnall, English Puritan clergyman (1616–79)**

'We find in Scripture a wide variety of style and language. There is a vast difference between the deeply emotional tenor of Hosea and the vividly descriptive manner of expression which characterizes Nahum; between the exhortations of Haggai and Hebrews, and the argumentations of Malachi and Galatians. Nevertheless, all are equally the Word of God.'
**William Hendriksen (1900–82)**

# Money

Silver shekels were the commonest form of currency, though gold and copper were also used. Coinage was gradually introduced into Judah under Persian influence from the late sixth century BC, though Jewish coins were only minted from the second century BC. The widow's 'mite' (penny) (Mark 12:42) is the only Jewish coin mentioned in the Bible but several Roman coins are included, particularly the denarius (Matthew 20:1–16; 22:19) which was roughly equivalent to the Greek drachma (Luke 15:8–9). Money can be used to build God's kingdom (Philippians 4:15–19), but it can also ensnare people (1 Timothy 6:10), and Jesus taught that people cannot trust God and money at the same time (Matthew 6:24).

# Plagues of Egypt

Mnemonic rhyme for the order of the plagues in Egypt:

**R**etaliating **f**or **g**reat **f**rustration **M**oses **b**adgered **h**ostile **l**eader **d**emanding **f**reedom

(River of blood, frogs, gnats, flies, malady (livestock), boils, hail, locusts, darkness, first-born)

'The book of books, the storehouse and magazine of life and comfort, the Holy Scriptures.'
**George Herbert, English poet (1593–1633)**

'Bibles laid open, millions of surprises.'
**George Herbert**

# Jewish calendar

| | | | |
|---|---|---|---|
| First month | Nisan or Abib | March/April | Esther 3:7 |
| Second month | Ziv or Iyyar | April/May | 1 Kings 6:37 |
| Third month | Sivan | May/June | Esther 8:9 |
| Fourth month | Tammuz | June/July | |
| Fifth month | Ab | July/August | |
| Sixth month | Elul | August/September | Nehemiah 6:15 |
| Seventh month | Ethanim or Tishri | September/October | 1 Kings 8:2 |
| Eighth month | Bul or Marchesvan | October/November | 1 Kings 6:38 |
| Ninth month | Kislev | November/December | Zechariah 7:1 |
| Tenth month | Tebeth | December/January | Esther 2:16 |
| Eleventh month | Shebat | January/February | Zechariah 1:7 |
| Twelfth month | Adar | February/March | Ezra 6:15 |

# Arts and crafts

Arts and crafts mentioned in the Bible include:

**Artistic skills**

| | |
|---|---|
| Dance | Jeremiah 31:13 |
| Embroidery | Exodus 26:36 |
| Engraving | 2 Chronicles 2:7 |
| Music | 1 Chronicles 6:31 |
| Weaving | Proverbs 31:19 |

**Building crafts**

| | |
|---|---|
| Carpentry | Mark 6:3 |
| Metalwork | Judges 17:4 |
| Pottery | Jeremiah 18:3 |
| Silversmith | Acts 19:24 |
| Stonemasonry | 1 Chronicles 14:1 |
| Tanning | Acts 10:32 |

'What you bring away from the Bible depends to some extend on what you carry to it.'
**Oliver Wendell Holmes, Sr., US writer (1809–94)**

'The Bible is a postgraduate course in the richest library of human experience.'
**Herbert Hoover, US president (1874–1964)**

'Lay hold on the Bible until the Bible lays hold on you.'
**William H. Houghton, US pastor, president of Moody Bible Institute (1887–1947)**

# Herbs and spices

Herbs and spices mentioned in the Bible include:

| | |
|---|---|
| Aloes | John 19:39 |
| Bitter herbs | Exodus 12:8 |
| Calamus | Song of Songs 4:14 |
| Cassia | Exodus 30:24 |
| Cinnamon | Exodus 30:23 |
| Cumin | Matthew 23:23 |
| Dill | Isaiah 28:25 |
| Frankincense | Matthew 2:11 |
| Galbanum | Exodus 30:34 |
| Garlic | Numbers 11:5 |
| Henna | Song of Songs 4:13 |
| Mint | Matthew 23:23 |
| Mustard | Luke 17:6 |
| Myrrh | Mark 15:23 |
| Nard | John 12:3 |
| Onycha | Exodus 30:34 |
| Rue | Luke 11:42 |
| Saffron | Song of Songs 4:14 |
| Stacte | Exodus 30:34 |

# Jewels and precious stones

Jewels and precious stones mentioned in the Bible include:

| | |
|---|---|
| Agate | Revelation 21:19 |
| Amethyst | Exodus 39:12 |
| Beryl | Revelation 21:20 |
| Carnelian | Ezekiel 28:13 |
| Chalcedony | Revelation 21:20 |
| Coral | Job 28:18 |
| Diamond | Exodus 28:18 |
| Emerald | Revelation 4:3 |
| Garnet | Exodus 28:17 |
| Jasper | Exodus 39:13 |
| Mother-of-pearl | Esther 1:6 |
| Onyx | Revelation 21:20 |
| Pearl | Matthew 13:45–6 |
| Quartz | Revelation 21:20 |
| Ruby | Exodus 39:10 |
| Sapphire | Ezekiel 1:26 |
| Topaz | Job 28:19 |
| Turquoise | Exodus 28:19 |

'England has two books, the Bible and Shakespeare. England made Shakespeare but the Bible made England.'
**Victor Hugo, French novelist (1802–85)**

'The Bible has been the *Magna Charta* of the poor and of the oppressed.'
**Thomas Henry Huxley, English biologist (1825–95)**

'That book is the rock on which our republic rests.'
**Andrew Jackson, US president (1767–1845)**

'Every Christian must refer always and everywhere to the Scriptures for all his choices, becoming like a child before it, seeking in it the most effective remedy against all his various weaknesses, and not daring to take a

# Feasts and festivals

| | | |
|---|---|---|
| Sabbath | | Exodus 20:8 |
| New moon | | Ezekiel 46:6 |
| Passover | Month 1, Day 14 | Leviticus 23:5 |
| Unleavened Bread | Month 1, Days 15–21 | Leviticus 23:6 |
| Harvest (Pentecost) | 50 days after harvest starts | Deuteronomy 16:9 |
| New Year | Month 7, Day 1 | Leviticus 23:23 |
| Day of Atonement | Month 7, Day 10 | Leviticus 23:26 |
| Shelters | Month 7, Day 15 | Leviticus 23:33; John 7:2 |
| Purim | Month 12, Days 14–15 | Esther 9:26 |

step without being illuminated by the divine rays of those words.'
**John Paul II, Polish Pope (Karol Wojtyla; 1920– )**

'The Holy Bible was the most important possession that our forebears placed aboard their ships as they embarked for the New World.'
**Lyndon B. Johnson, US president (1908–73)**

'The Bible is the greatest benefit which the human race has ever experienced.'
**Immanuel Kant, German philosopher (1724–1804)**

'On the Day of Judgement you will not be asked, "What did you read?" but "What did you do?"'
**Thomas à Kempis, German monk (Thomas Hemmerken; c. 1380–1471)**

'When you read God's word, you must constantly be saying to yourself, "It is talking to me, and about me."'
**Søren Kierkegaard, Danish philosopher (1813–55)**

'In all my perplexities and distresses the Bible has never failed to give me light and strength.'
**Robert E. Lee, US army general (1807–70)**

'This great book ... is the best gift God has given to man ... But for it we could not know right from wrong.'
**Abraham Lincoln, US president (1809–65)**

'All that I am I owe to Jesus Christ, revealed to me in His divine Book.'
**David Livingstone, Scottish medical missionary (1813–73)**

# Food and drink

Food and drink mentioned in the Bible include:

**Cereal**

| | |
|---|---|
| Barley | John 6:13 |
| Corn | Isaiah 55:1 |
| Millet | Ezekiel 4:9 |
| Spelt | Ezekiel 4:9 |
| Wheat | Ruth 2:23 |

**Meat and fish**

| | |
|---|---|
| Beef | Deuteronomy 14:26 |
| Calf | Luke 15:30 |
| Chicken | Nehemiah 5:18 |
| Deer | Deuteronomy 12:15 |
| Fish | John 21:10 |
| Goat | Judges 13:15 |
| Lamb | 2 Samuel 12:4 |
| Ox | Nehemiah 5:18 |
| Quail | Numbers 11:31–34 |
| Veal | Amos 6:4 |
| Venison | Deuteronomy 14:5 |

**Fruit**

| | |
|---|---|
| Almonds | Genesis 43:11 |
| Apple | Song of Songs 2:5 |
| Dates | Song of Songs 7:7 |
| Fig | Mark 11:14 |
| Grapes | Leviticus 19:10 |
| Melon | Jeremiah 10:5 |
| Nuts | Genesis 43:11 |
| Pomegranate | Song of Songs 6:11 |
| Raisins | 1 Chronicles 12:40 |

**Vegetables**

| | |
|---|---|
| Beans | Genesis 25:29 |
| Cucumbers | Isaiah 1:8 |
| Garlic | Numbers 11:5 |
| Leeks | Numbers 11:5 |
| Onions | Numbers 11:5 |
| Peas | 2 Samuel 17:28 |

**Other foods**

| | |
|---|---|
| Bread | John 6:11 |
| Butter | Proverbs 30:33 |
| Cheese, cream | 2 Samuel 17:18 |
| Egg | Luke 11:12 |
| Honey | Mark 1:6 |
| Mustard | Matthew 13:31 |
| Olive oil | Ezekiel 16:13 |
| Salt | Mark 9:50 |

**Drink**

| | |
|---|---|
| Beer | Deuteronomy 29:6 |
| Milk | Isaiah 55:1 |
| Water | John 4:17 |
| Wine | Matthew 26:29 |

'The Bible ... transcends all our categories and increasingly supplies our finite minds from its inexhaustible store of treasures.'
**D. Martyn Lloyd-Jones, Welsh preacher and writer (1899–1981)**

'Every word in the Bible points to Christ.'
**Martin Luther, German monk and theologian (1483–1546)**

# Armour and weapons

Armour and weapons mentioned in the Bible include:

**Armour**

| | |
|---|---|
| Coat of armour | 1 Samuel 17:38 |
| Helmet | Isaiah 59:17 |
| Shield | 1 Samuel 17:7 |

**Weapons**

| | |
|---|---|
| Axe | Psalm 35:3 |
| Bow and arrow | Jeremiah 50:29 |
| Club | Proverbs 25:18 |
| Dagger | 1 Kings 18:28 |
| Javelin | 1 Samuel 17:45 |
| Lance | Job 41:26 |
| Sling | 1 Samuel 17:40 |
| Spear | John 19:34 |
| Sword | Isaiah 17:39 |

'The Bible is alive, it speaks to me; it has feet, it runs after me; it has hands, it lays hold on me.'
**Martin Luther**

'The Bible is not antique, or modern. It is eternal.'
**Martin Luther**

'To read without faith is to walk in darkness.'
**Martin Luther**

'The Bible is not a ladder but a foundation.'
**John Gresham Machen, US scholar and churchman (1881–1937)**

'Read the Bible, not as a newspaper, but as a home letter. If a cluster of heavenly fruit hangs within reach, gather it. If a promise lies upon the page as a blank check, cash it. If a prayer is recorded, appropriate it, and launch it as a feathered arrow from the bow of your desire. If an example of holiness gleams before you, ask God to do as much for you. If the truth is revealed in all its intrinsic splendour, entreat that its brilliance may ever irradiate the hemisphere of your life.'
**F.B. Meyer, English preacher and author (1847–1929)**

'Sin will keep you from this Book. This Book will keep you from sin.'
**Dwight L. Moody, US evangelist (1837–99)**

'The Bible is a storehouse of whose contents no one can afford to be ignorant. It repays reading and study whether it be approached merely because of its literary value, or its ethical teachings, or its practical bearing on everyday life.'
**Dwight L. Moody**

# Clothing

Clothing mentioned in the Bible include:

**Men's clothing**

| | |
|---|---|
| Belt | Acts 12:8 |
| Cap | Daniel 3:21 |
| Cloak | Mark 6:56 |
| Coat | Matthew 5:40 |
| Linen shorts | Jeremiah 13:1 |
| Robes | Luke 20:46 |
| Sandals | Exodus 3:5 |
| Shirt | Luke 9:3 |
| Tassels | Numbers 15:23 |
| Turban | Proverbs 1:9 |

**Women's clothing**

| | |
|---|---|
| Cape | Song of Songs 5:7 |
| Coat | Ezekiel 16:8 |
| Dresses | 1 Peter 3:3 |
| Embroidered gown | Ezekiel 16:10 |
| Hat | Isaiah 3:20 |
| Jewellery | Jeremiah 2:32 |
| Linen garments | Proverbs 31:24 |
| Silk cloak | Ezekiel 16:10 |
| Veil | Isaiah 3:20 |

'If a problem exists, the Bible has something to say about it.'
**George Campbell Morgan, English Bible teacher and writer (1863–1945)**

'The Scriptures were not given to increase our knowledge, but to change our lives.'
**Dwight L. Moody**

'What does not agree with Scripture does not come from God.'
**Leon L. Morris, Australian Bible lecturer, preacher and author (1914– )**

'The vigour of our spiritual life will be in exact proportion to the place held by the Bible in our life and thoughts.'
**George Müller, Prussian born founder of a Bristol orphanage (1805–98)**

'I read my Bible to know what people ought to do, and my newspaper to know what they are doing.'
**Cardinal John Henry Newman, English theologian (1801–90)**

'No sciences are better attested than the religion of the Bible.'
**Sir Isaac Newton, English scientist (1642–1727)**

'Some books are copper, some are silver, and some few are gold; but the Bible alone is like a book all made up of bank notes.'
**John Newton, English hymn and letter writer (1725–1807)**

# Diseases and illnesses

Diseases and illnesses in the Bible include:

| | |
|---|---|
| Blindness | John 9:3 |
| Boils | Exodus 9:9 |
| Deafness | Luke 7:22 |
| Dumbness | Matthew 15:30 |
| Epilepsy | Matthew 4:24 |
| Fever | Job 30:30 |
| Haemorrhaging | Matthew 9:20 |
| Lameness | Acts 14:8 |
| Mental illness | Daniel 4:36 |
| Paralysis | Matthew 9:2 |
| Skin disease ('leprosy') | Luke 17:12 |
| Tumours | 1 Samuel 5:6 |

'One of the many divine qualities of the Bible is this, that it does not yield its secrets to the irreverent and the censorious.'
**James I. Packer, English theologian (1926– )**

'To defer to God's Word is an act of faith; any querying and editing of it on our own initiative is an exhibition of unbelief.'
**James I. Packer**

'I have found ... that once one gets to grips with the actual stuff of the New Testament, its vitality is astonishing.

I found myself provoked, challenged, stimulated, comforted and generally convicted of my previous shallow knowledge of Holy Scripture. The centuries seemed to melt away and here was I confronted by eternal truths which my soul, however reluctantly, felt bound to accept.'
**J.B. Phillips, English Bible translator, author and broadcaster (1906–82)**

'I never had any doubt about it being of divine origin ... point out to me any similar collection of writings that has lasted for as many thousands of years and is still a best-seller, world-wide. It had to be of divine origin.'
**Ronald Reagan, US president (1911– )**

'The more effectively we analyze a Bible passage, the more readily the message it actually contains reveals itself and the less we have to struggle to "find" a message hidden within it.'
**John Richardson, Anglican chaplain to the University of East London**

'A thorough knowledge of the Bible is worth more than a college education.'
**Theodore Roosevelt, US president (1858–1919)**

# Bible words

The number of occurrences of a
selection of Bible words in the *Good
News Bible*:

*angel* and associated words 356
    *angel* 245, *angels* 111
*anger* 278
*authority* 113
*believe* and associated words 303
    *believe* 201, *believed* 72, *believes*
    20, *believing* 10
*blessing* and associated words 141
    *blessing* 84, *blessings* 57
*Christ* see Jesus
*church* 88
*death* and associated words 1405
    *death* 625, *die* 436, *died* 306,
    *dies* 38
*eternal* 139
*faith* and associated words 458
    *faith* 277, *faithful* 145, *faithfulness*
    36
*family* and associated words 460
    *family* 317, *families* 143
*fear* and associated words 450
    *afraid* 314, *fear* 131, *fearful* 1,
    *fears* 4
*fellowship* 83
*fool* and associated words 139
    *fool* 68, *foolish* 71
*forgive* and associated words 198
    *forgive* 112, *forgives* 8, *forgiven*
    67, *forgiveness* 11
*free* and associated words 230
    *free* 203, *freedom* 27

*friend* and associated words 228
    *friend* 75, *friends* 141, *friendship*
    12
*Gentiles* 118
*gift* and associated words 207
    *gift* 109, *gifts* 98
*give* and associated words 1841
    *give* 1110, *gives* 185, *given* 546
*glory* and associated words 251
    *glory* 206, *glorious* 45
*God* 4165
*good* and associated words 832
    *good* 790, *goodness* 42
*gospel* and associated words 162
    *gospel* 53, *good news* 109
*grace* and associated words 111
    *grace* 104, *gracious* 7
*happy* and associated words 272
    *happy* 226, *happiness* 46
*hate* and associated words 184
    *hate* 134, *hates* 39, *hatred* 11
*heart* and associated words 297
    *heart* 204, *hearts* 91, *heartfelt* 2
*heaven* 399
*hell* 21
*help* and associated words 525
    *help* 508, *helps* 15, *helpful* 2
*holy* 565
    *holy* 549, *holiness* 16
*Holy Spirit* 102
    *Spirit* 280, *spirit* 143
*hope* and associated words 181
    *hope* 171, *hopes* 10
*humble* and associated words 67
    *humble* 59, *humility* 8

*idol* and associated words 281
  *idol* 48, *idols* 2219, *idolatry* 14
*Israel* and associated words 2287
  *Israel* 1796, *Israelites* 491
*Jesus* 1642
  *Christ* 511, *Jesus Christ* 137
*joy* and associated words 241
  *joy* 198, *joyful* 32, *joyfully* 7, *joyous* 1,
    *overjoyed* 3
*judgement* and associated words 240
  *judge* 152, *judgement* 88
*justice* 104
*Kingdom of God* 63
*knowledge* 101
*law* and associated words 483
  *law* 478, *lawful* 1, *lawless* 4
*lie* and associated words (both
falsehood and posture) 177
  *lie* 108, *lied* 4, *lying* 65
*life* 665
*light* 232
*love* and associated words 765
  *love* 617, *loved* 74, *loves* 58, *loving*
    13, *lovingly* 1, *beloved* 2
*man* and associated words 2482
  *man* 1304, *men* 1178
*mercy* and associated words 208
  *mercy* 134, *merciful* 74
*minister* 2
*miracle* and associated words 126
  *miracle* 28, *miracles* 98
*money* 203
*neighbour* and associated words 52
  *neighbour* 22, *neighbours* 30
*obey* and associated words 553
  *obey* 437, *obeyed* 98, *obeys* 18
*offering* and associated words 767

offering 448, offerings 319
*peace* and associated words 257
  *peace* 244, *peaceful* 13
*perfect* and associated words 56
  *perfect* 54, *perfection* 2
*poor* and associated words 225
  *poor* 214, *poverty* 11
*power* and associated words 625
  *power* 503, *powerful* 122
*praise* 375
*praises* 28
*pray* and associated words 518
  *pray* 198, *prayed* 115, *prays* 8,
    *prayer* 126, *prayers* 71
*preach* and associated words 145
  *preach* 52, *preached* 52, *preaches*
    4, *preaching* 37
*pride* 54
*promise* and associated words 572
  *promise* 262, *promised* 247,
    *promises* 63
*prophet* and associated words 528
  *prophet* 258, *prophets* 270
*proud* 126
*punish* and associated words 535
  *punish* 278, *punished* 131,
    *punishes* 21, *punishment* 105
*pure* and associated words 114
  *pure* 109, *purity* 5
*reject* and associated words 146
  *reject* 51, *rejected* 88, *rejects* 7
*rest* and associated words 286
  *rest* 271, *rested* 14, *rests* 1
*rich* and associated words 227
  *rich* 191, *riches* 36
*righteous* and associated words 218
  *righteous* 164, *righteousness* 54

*ritual* and associated words 61
  *ritual* 58, *rituals* 3
*Sabbath* and associated words 136
  *Sabbath* 126, *Sabbaths* 10
*sacrifice* 171
*salvation* 53
*Satan* 45
*save* and associated words 515
  *save* 311, *saved* 156, *saves* 48
*Saviour/saviour* 49
*service* and associated words 95
  *service* 88, *services* 7
*sin* and associated words 1028
  *sin* 432, *sinned* 146, *sins* 403,
  *sinful* 47
*sorrow* and associated words 59
  *sorrow* 58, *sorrowful* 1
*Spirit* see Holy Spirit
*strong* and associated words 401
  *strong* 221, *strength* 158,
  *strengthen* 22
*suffer* and associated words 267
  *suffer* 111, *suffered* 43, *suffers* 3,
  *suffering* 110
*teach* and associated words 494
  *teach* 146, *teacher* 80, *teachers*
  84, *teaching* 128, *teachings* 56

*time* 1132
*truth* and associated words 209
  *truth* 206, *truthful* 3
*understand* and associated words 187
  *understand* 142, *understanding* 45
*victory* and associated words 201
  *victory* 175, *victorious* 26
*vow* and associated words 97
  *vow* 80, *vowed* 7, *vows* 10
*war* and associated words 207
  *war* 198, *wars* 9
*water* and associated words 518
  *water* 477, *waters* 41
*weak* and associated words 125
  *weak* 120, *weakness* 5
*wisdom* 196
*wise* 184
*woman* and associated words 689
  *woman* 396, *women* 293
*work* and associated words 536
  *work* 435, *worked* 70, *worker* 8,
  *works* 23
*world* and associated words 515
  *world* 507, *worldly* 8
*worry* and associated words 46
  *worry* 33, *worried* 13
*worship* 510

'The Bible is the one Book to which any thoughtful man may go with any honest question of life or destiny and find the answer of God by honest searching.'
**John Ruskin, English art critic and author (1819–1900)**

'There's a Bible on that shelf there. But I keep it next to Voltaire – poison and antidote.'
**Bertrand Russell, English philosopher (1872–1970)**

'A Bible-reading laity is a nation's surest defence against error.'
**J.C. Ryle, English evangelical, Anglican Bishop of Liverpool (1816–1900)**

'We must read our Bibles like men digging for hidden treasure.'
**J.C. Ryle**

'The deity of Christ is the key doctrine of the Scriptures. Reject it, and the Bible becomes a jumble of words without any unifying theme. Accept it, and the Bible becomes an intelligible and ordered revelation of God in the person of Jesus Christ.'
**J. Oswald Sanders, New Zealand missionary and Bible teacher (1902–92)**

'The ordinary Christian with the Bible in his hand can say that the majority is wrong.'
**Francis Schaeffer, US theologian (1912–84)**

'No book presents morals in such inextricable union with politics as the Bible.'
**John Robert Seeley, English historian (1834–95)**

'Read it to get the facts, study it to get the meaning, meditate on it to get the benefit.'
**David Sheppard, Bishop of Liverpool (1929–  )**

'If we made the practice of selecting daily some short portion of Scripture for our meditation throughout the day, the most ignorant among us would soon attain a knowledge which at present appears far beyond his reach.'
**Charles Simeon, English evangelical clergyman (1759–1836)**

'Defend the Bible? I would just as soon defend a lion. Just turn the Bible loose. It will defend itself.'
**Charles Haddon Spurgeon, English Baptist preacher (1834–92)**

'The Bible is a vein of pure gold, unalloyed by quartz or any earthly substance. This is a star without a speck; a sun without a blot; a light without darkness; a moon without its paleness; a glory without a dimness. O Bible! It cannot be said of any other book that it is perfect and pure; but of thee we can declare all wisdom is gathered up in thee, without a particle of folly. This is the judge that ends the strife, where wit and reason fail. This is the book untainted by any error; but is pure, unalloyed, perfect truth.'
**Charles Haddon Spurgeon**

'The Bible, the whole Bible, and nothing but the Bible is the religion of Christ's church.'
**Charles Haddon Spurgeon**

'The Bible has the authority of God because God himself has spoken ... I do not believe that there could be a more authentic or authoritative witness to the historic Jesus.'
**John Stott, Anglican author and leader (1921– )**

'There is a living God. He has spoken in the Bible. He means what he says and will do all he has promised.'
**James Hudson Taylor, English medical missionary (1832–1905)**

'The truly wise man is he who always believes the Bible against the opinion of any man.'
**R.A. Torrey, US evangelist, pastor and author (1856–1928)**

'God did not write a book and send it by messenger to be read at a distance by unaided minds. He spoke a book and lives in his spoken words, constantly speaking his words and causing the power of them to persist across the years.'
**A.W. Tozer, pastor, author and editor (1897–1963)**

'We must never edit God.'
**A.W. Tozer**

'Most people are bothered by those passages in Scripture which they cannot understand; but as for me, I always noticed that the passages in Scripture which trouble me most are those that I do understand.'
**Mark Twain, US author (Samuel Langhorne Clemens; 1835–1910)**

'Jesus loves me – this I know, For the Bible tells me so.'
**Anna Bartlett Warner, US writer (1820–1915)**

'It is impossible to rightly govern the world without God and the Bible.'
**George Washington, US president (1732–99)**

'It is one thing to be told that the Bible has authority because it is divinely inspired, and another thing to feel one's heart leap out and grasp its truth.'
**Leslie Weatherhead, English author and minister (1893–1976)**

'The Bible is a book of faith, and a book of doctrine, and a book of morals, and a book of religion, of especial revelation from God.'
**Daniel Webster, US statesman (1782–1852)**

'All the knowledge you want is comprised in one book, the Bible.'
**John Wesley, English preacher and co-founder of Methodism (1703–91)**

# Psalm 119

Psalm 119 is devoted to the praise of God's Word, which is mentioned in every verse except verses 121 and 122. Probably if we were to substitute 'will' for 'Word' (or its equivalent), we should not be far wrong. The earnest desire of the writer was that his will should be brought into blessed and unbroken union with the divine purpose in his life.

In its structure the psalm is an elaborate acrostic. In the original, each verse in a given section begins with the same letter, so that the twenty-two sections present the complete Hebrew alphabet.

It needs to be often used to be understood and valued. Chrysostom, Ambrose, Augustine, and Luther have left on record high tributes to its worth. There are several key expressions, which recur again and again, such as 'quicken' and 'teach me thy statutes'. It is interesting also, to construct the psalmist's biography from his confessions. He had gone astray like a lost sheep, was small and despised, had many adversaries, was like a bottle in the smoke; but he accounted God's will and service more than food or gold, and his one desire was to be taught to do that will.

**F.B. Meyer**, *Devotional Commentary*

'I am sorry for men who do not read the Bible every day. I wonder why they deprive themselves of the strength and pleasure.'
**Thomas Woodrow Wilson, US president (1856–1924)**

'When you read the Bible you will know that it is the word of God, because you will have found it the key to your own heart, your own happiness, your own duty.'
**Thomas Woodrow Wilson**

'The Bible is for the government of the people, by the people, and for the people.'
**John Wycliffe, English religious reformer (c. 1329–84)**

# The power of the Bible

## Bill's Bible

This is a story of how God's Word survived one of the most intense fires ever to burn on a US naval warship.

On Friday, 14th May 1987 Barbara Kiser bade farewell to her husband Bill. He waved from the deck of the USS *Stark* as the frigate eased out from its jetty at Mina Sulman, in the port of Bahrain. As the ship cut into the still blue waters of the Gulf, the couple exchanged their last wave in the form of the sign language message, 'I love you'.

At the Kisers' own expense Barbara and four-year-old John had moved to Bahrain and rented a flat to be near Bill. All three looked forward to Bill's brief periods of shore leave, but little did they know that this one would be his last.

In the gathering dusk on Sunday 16th May, a lone Iraqi pilot guided his plane south east down the Gulf, hugging the Saudi Arabian coast. North of Bahrain the *Stark* cruised in the twilight, the sailors on deck watching the sun slowly slide into tranquil waters.

Suddenly the Iraqi pilot noticed a dot on his radar. Sharply banking towards the east he took aim, probably thinking his target was an oil tanker. Two deadly accurate Exocet missiles were unleashed before the pilot set a course for home.

Lieutenant William Kiser was in his quarter when the missiles struck. One exploded, causing a raging inferno which killed him and thirty-six other sailors, while the other missile tore straight through the ship.

On hearing the tragic news, Barbara remembered the verse in Job, 'The LORD gave, and the LORD hath taken away; blessed be the name of the LORD' (1:21, AV). She resolved to show a spirit of forgiveness by sending a Bible to the Iraqi pilot. By the time this had been arranged through the American Embassy, the stricken *Stark* was back in Bahrain.

Clutching a torch, Barbara was allowed to see her husband's quarters. Amongst the blackness of tangled metal, flooded decks and charred debris, Barbara found what she was looking for – Bill's Bible. God's word had endured the blazing inferno.

Barbara believes that through the power of the Holy Spirit which enabled her to forgive the Iraqi pilot and send him a Bible as an expression of that forgiveness, God allowed her to recover the only surviving possession of her husband – Bill's Bible.

## Stanley's last book

When Henry Morton Stanley started across the continent of Africa, he had 73 books, but as the journey continued through the days and weeks he was obliged to throw away the books one by one, until they were all gone but his Bible. It is said that he read it through three times on that remarkable trip in search of the missionary David Livingstone in the heart of Africa.

## Comfort in death

'He [Sir Walter Scott] expressed a wish that I should read to him and when I asked him from what book, he said, "Need you ask? There is but one." I chose the 14th chapter of St John's Gospel; he listened with mild attention and said when I had done: "Well, this is a great comfort – I have followed you distinctly, and I feel as if I were yet to be myself again."' (Lockhart, *The Life of Sir Walter Scott.*)

## God still speaks

'I only wish to let a wild, warm enthusiasm flow from my heart down my arm to flood from my pen on to the paper. Bible study has torn apart my life and remade it. That is to say that God, through his word, has done so. In the darkest periods of my life when everything seemed hopeless, I would struggle in the grey dawns of many faraway countries to grasp the basic truths of Scripture passages. I looked for no immediate answers to my problems. Only did I sense intuitively that I was drinking drafts from a fountain that gave life to my soul.

'Slowly as I grappled with textual and theological problems, a strength grew deep within me. Foundations cemented themselves to an other-worldly rock beyond the reach of time and space, and I became strong and more alive. If I could write poetry about it I would. If I could sing through paper, I would flood your

# The Bible in action

The Bible itself gives us several pictures of what it does. The Bible is like:

- **a judge** (Hebrews 4:12), discerning our intentions and what is in our inner beings;
- **a shower or drops of rain** (Deuteronomy 32:2; 2 Samuel 23:2–4), to refresh and revive us;
- **a seed** (Luke 8:11), to produce fruit in our lives;
- **a sword** (Ephesians 6:17; Hebrews 4:12), to pierce sharply – by convicting and converting, or condemning;
- **a hammer** (Jeremiah 23:29), to crack open rock-like hearts and to fashion our lives sensitively and smoothly;
- **a fire** (Jeremiah 20:9; 23:29), to powerfully destroy what is wrong in our lives and to refine us;
- **a lamp** (Psalm 119:105), to dispel the darkness of sin and to guide us through life;
- **a mirror** (James 1:22–25), to reveal and reflect what we are truly like;
- **food** – milk (1 Corinthians 3:2; 1 Peter 2:2), solid food (Hebrews 5:12–14), bread (Matthew 4:4), to provide us with spiritual sustenance all our days as God's people.

soul with the glorious melodies that express what I have found. I cannot exaggerate for there are no expressions majestic enough to tell of the glory I have seen or of the wonder of finding that I, a neurotic, unstable, middle-aged man have my feet firmly planted in eternity and breathe the air of heaven. And all this has come to me through a careful study of Scripture.' (John White, author and psychiatrist.)

## The best book

'I put a New Testament among your books for the very same reasons and with the very same hopes that made me write an easy account of it for you when you were a little child – because it is the best book that ever was or will be known in the world, and because it teaches you the best lessons by which

> **'Accept … the word of God as the sword which the Spirit gives you.'**
>
> Paul, in Ephesians 6:17 (GNB)

any human creature who tries to be truthful and faithful to duty can possibly be guided.' (Charles Dickens, writing to his youngest son, who was leaving home to join his brother in Australia.)

## High explosives

'The Bible is a high explosive. It works in strange ways and no living man can tell or know how the book in its journey through the world has startled the individual soul in ten thousand different places into a new life, a new belief, a new conception, a new faith. (Stanley Baldwin, British prime minister.)

## Royal standards

In his book, *Through the Valley of the Kwai*, Ernest Gordon tells of the amazing transformation that took place in a Japanese prisoner-of-war camp in Burma between Christmas 1942 and Christmas 1943. In 1942 the camp was a sea of mud and filth. It was a scene of gruelling, sweated labour and brutal treatment by the Japanese guards. There was hardly any food, and the law that pervaded the whole camp was the law of the jungle – every man for himself. Twelve months later, the ground of the camp was cleared and clean. The bamboo bed slats had been de-bugged. Green boughs had been used to rebuild the huts and on Christmas morning 2,000 men were at worship. What had happened? During the year a prisoner had shared his last crumb of food with another man who was also in desperate need. Then he had died. Amongst his belongings they found a Bible. Could this be the secret of his life, of his willingness to give to others and not to grasp for himself? One by one the prisoners began to read it. Soon the Spirit of God began to grip their hearts and change their lives, and in a period of less than twelve months there was a spiritual and moral revolution within that camp. It was lifted from disgrace to dignity by the royal standards of the word of God. *When the Bible begins to be lived, men begin to be lifted.* God's word is royal in its source, its subjects and its standards.

## The lively oracles of God

During the British Coronation ceremony a Bible is presented to the monarch with the words: 'We present you with this book, the most valuable thing that this world affords. Here is wisdom. This is the royal law. These are the lively oracles of God.'

# God spoke to them through the book of Romans

## Augustine

It was the summer of 386 AD. Augustine was sitting in a friend's garden in Milan. He was in tears because he lacked the will to break with the old life and begin the new. He despaired of himself. He heard a child's voice crying, 'Tolle, lege; tolle, lege' ('Take up and read; take up and read'). Without delay Augustine took up his copy of a Latin version of Paul's letters that lay on a bench beside him and read Romans 13:13–14, the first words on which his eyes fell. He read no further than, 'Clothe yourselves with the Lord Jesus Christ, and do not think about how to gratify the desires of the sinful nature.' Augustine later wrote, 'As I finished the sentence, the light of confidence flooded into my heart and all the darkness of doubt vanished.' Augustine became one of the greatest leaders of the Christian Church.

## Martin Luther

In the early 16th century, Martin Luther, an Augustinian monk and a professor at the University of Wittenberg, yearned and craved for peace with God. In 1515–16 Luther thought deeply about Romans 1:17 and the phrase 'the righteousness of God'. He 'did not yet understand Paul's words in Romans that the gospel is the saving power of God to everyone who believes in Christ, *because* it reveals the righteousness of God. This righteousness of God is nothing other than Christ's perfect obedience to his Father's will in life and death, "even the death of the cross" – obedience which God counts as belonging to all those in whose place Christ died. Just as the punishment of the believer's sin was borne by Christ so it is because of Christ's righteousness that the same believer, though ungodly in himself, is pronounced "just" or righteous in the sight of God. In this way, Paul says, faith receives the righteousness of God: "To him that worketh not, but believeth on him that justifies the ungodly, his faith is counted for righteousness" (Romans 4:5).

'When the Holy Spirit revealed this to Luther, and he learned that it was by faith alone that he could be saved, and not by his own good works, the light of the truth shone with such brilliance, and brought such deliverance into his spirit, that he felt Paul's words, "The just shall live by faith", were the very gate of paradise itself. And so this great truth, *The just shall live by faith* (Romans 1:17) became the fundamental truth of the Reformation. In other words, a wonderful reformation came personally to Luther before God used him as the instrument of the Reformation in Europe.' (S. M. Houghton.)

## John Wesley

On 24th May 1738, Luther's introduction to Romans was being read at a meeting in London. In the audience was a young man named John Wesley. He was a clergyman and missioner to Georgia, and was very interested by what he heard at that meeting. Wesley wrote in his diary, 'In the evening I went very unwillingly to a society in Aldersgate Street, where one was reading Luther's preface to the Epistle to the Romans. About a quarter before nine, while he was describing the change which God works in the heart through faith in Christ, I felt my heart strangely warmed. I felt I did trust in Christ, Christ alone, for salvation. And an assurance was given me that he had taken away *my* sins, even *mine*, and saved *me* from the law of sin and death.' John Wesley was later able to speak to countless people and bring many to a living faith in Jesus.

# The power of God's word

Crossing to the north of India in a caravan, a godly missionary stooping over an exhausted Indian who had been left to perish, whispered in his ear, 'Brother, what is your hope?' Lifting himself with a great effort, the man replied, 'The blood of Jesus Christ cleanseth us from all sin' (1 John 1:7), and expired with the effort. Amazed at the answer of an apparent heathen, the missionary observed a piece of paper grasped tightly in the hand of the dead man: it was a single leaf of the Bible, the first chapter of John's First Epistle. One page only had converted this man and made him into a temple of the Holy Ghost.

# 'Confronted by eternal truths'

'I have found ... that once one gets to grips with the actual stuff of the New Testament, its vitality is astonishing. I found myself provoked, challenged, stimulated, comforted and generally convicted of my previous shallow knowledge of Holy Scripture. The centuries seemed to melt away and here was I confronted by eternal truths which my soul, however reluctantly, felt bound to accept.' (J. B. Phillips, Bible translator.)

# In solitary confinement ... but not alone

Martin Niemöller was incarcerated in a Nazi concentration camp for many years, but was allowed the Bible as his one possession. He wrote: 'The Bible: what did this book mean to me during the long and weary years of solitary confinement and then for the last four years at the Dachau cell-building? The word of God was simply everything to me – comfort and strength, guidance and hope, master of my days and companion of my nights, the bread which kept me from starvation, and the water of life which refreshed my soul. And even more, "solitary confinement" ceased to be solitary.' This is the constant experience of those who have dared to take God at his word, despite all the odds against them.

---

**'The Bible is alive, it speaks to me; it has feet, it runs after me; it has hands, it lays hold on me.'**

Martin Luther, German Reformation leader (1483–1546)

---

# A hymn on the Bible

Lord, Thy Word abideth,
And our footsteps guideth;
Who its truth believeth
Light and joy receiveth.

When our foes are near us,
They Thy Word doth cheer us,
Word of consolation,
Message of salvation.

When the storms are o'er us,
And dark clouds before us,
Then its light directeth,
And our way protecteth.

Who can tell the pleasure,
Who recount the treasure,
By Thy Word imparted,
To the simple-hearted?

Word of mercy, giving
Succour to the living;
Word of life, supplying
Comfort to the dying!

O that we, discerning
Its most holy learning,
Lord, may love and fear Thee,
Evermore be near Thee!

Henry Williams Baker, 1821–77

# The buried Bibles of Madagascar

In 1834 missionaries of the London Missionary Society built a new printing-house, and took other means to help the work of Scripture publication; and in the same year they issued a reading-book which contained extracts from the Scriptures. In 1835, however, a great persecution broke out. A royal edict, forbidding Christianity and making the possession of Christian books punishable by death, was issued in March 1835. At that time, the section Ezekiel-Malachi and part of Job remained to be printed, and the missionaries resolved not to leave the country until they had placed the first complete Bible in the hands of their converts. Though deprived of Malagasy help they finished their task by means of hard work in June of the same year, and distributed among the Christians copies of the whole Bible, made up of the various portions of the Old Testament published between 1831 and 1835, and the New Testament of 1830.

Before the last missionaries left the island in July 1836, they had also, for greater security, buried in the earth 70 copies of the whole Bible, and stored in various hiding places several cases of New Testaments, the Psalms, and other portions. One copy of the 'buried Bibles' was used during 'the killing times' by a small community of Christians at Fihaonana in the province of Vonizongo, and was kept for greater security in a cave which had been used as a smallpox hospital – the same cave where Razaka, who afterwards became a notable leader in the church, lay hidden for over two years. The volume was carefully repaired and sewn with thread and vegetable fibre, and was protected with a cover of skin.

The 'buried Bibles', which passed stealthily from hand to hand, and were read in secret and at the risk of the owners' lives, became the fuel that kept the fire of holy faith burning during a quarter of a century of severe persecution. When the missionaries returned in 1862, they found that the little band of Malagasy Christians had grown from 200 to over 2,000.

# Lord Shaftesbury, social reformer

The study of the sacred Scriptures was always a delight to Lord Shaftesbury, and never more so than in these last years of his life. A Bible was always at hand in his library, and nothing more remarkably exemplified the retention of his faculties than the manner in which, whenever a reference to the Scriptures was necessary, he could, in a moment, turn to chapter and verse.

There are many references in the Diary to his biblical studies at this period, two of which we quote:

*1 April, Good Friday.* Let our first thought be that of St Paul: 'I determined to know nothing but Jesus Christ, and him crucified' (1 Corinthians 2:2). It is very remarkable; he says not *no one*, but *no thing.* He excludes thus every possible adjunct of man's hope or invention; every shadow of good deeds and selfrighteousness; every notion, however small, of something besides Christ.

*31 August.* Day opens beautifully; rose at half-past five, with every promise of comfort for the day. Psalms and Proverbs. How deeply evangelical is that Book of Proverbs! How plainly one may see and feel Christ speaking under the Old as under the New Testament!

## The experience of a Bible translator

As one New Testament scholar wrote, 'I became so absorbed in the study of the word that on one occasion when someone declared, "Time to eat," I was unable to determine whether it was time for the noon meal or for the evening meal ... to describe the joy one feels in contributing to the

communication of God's word is difficult. For example, the love chapter, 1 Corinthians 13, consumed hours of discussion and study, but it was all worthwhile ... for one phrase that emerged from the Greek, not found in other translations, love "always protects" (1 Corinthians 13:7).' (*The Story of the New International Version.*)

## William Wilberforce, the liberator

William Wilberforce (1759–1833) was strikingiy converted at the age of 25. In a life spent chiefly in political activities, he maintained an unblemished Christian walk for half a century. His chief efforts were directed to the ending of the infamous slave trade and of slavery in the British Empire. The former was ended in 1807 and the latter in 1833 at a cost to the British Government of £20,000,000. The knowledge that this had been done caused Wilberforce to die happy 'Few men,' it has been said, 'achieved more for the benefit of mankind.'

William Wilberforce was also involved in the formation of the British and Foreign Bible Society. Early in 1803 ... Wilberforce's diary records a breakfast-party with three friends 'on Bible Society formation'.

A few days later the discussion was resumed at the counting-house of Mr Hardcastle, a city friend, near Swan Stairs on Thames-side; and by the light of candles – so dark was that April morning – the little group decided on the inauguration of the Society, with Lord Teignmouth [formerly Governor-General of India] as its first president. It was destined to do much more and go much further than its founders ever dreamed.

# Tears mixed with ink

When Handel's servant brought him his morning refreshment, 'he often stood silent with astonishment to see his master's tears mixing with the ink as he penned his divine compositions.' And a friend, calling upon the great musician when in the act of setting those pathetic words, 'He was despised and rejected of men' (Isaiah 53:3) found him absolutely sobbing.

# Thoroughly equipped

'Preparing for a long trip, the young Christian said to his friend, "I am just about packed. I only have to put in a guidebook, a lamp, a mirror, a microscope, a telescope, a volume of fine poetry, a few biographies, a package of old letters, a book of songs, a sword, a hammer, and a set of books I have been studying."

"But," the friend objected, "you can't get all that into your bag."

"Oh, yes," replied the young man, "it doesn't take much room." He placed his Bible in the comer of the suitcase and closed the lid.' (*The Employment Counselor*.)

# The Bible as inspiration

The Bible has been the inspiration for innumerable works of art in the form of music, poetry, paintings, sculptures, stained-glass windows, illustrated books, etc. Below is a sample of this vast range.

## Music

Over the years many types of music have been inspired including:

### Gregorian chant

This is plainsong – the unaccompanied voice. This was popular in the 6th century and was so called because Pope Gregory I (540–604) refashioned the liturgy. Recently it has experienced a revival with recordings in the popular musical charts.

### Great orchestral pieces

These include:

*Coronation Anthem*, with its famous anthem 'Zadok the Priest', George Frederick Handel (1685–1759)

*Elijah*, Felix Mendelssohn (1809–47), words selected by Julius Schrubring

*Esther*, George Frederick Handel, words by Pelham Humfrey (1647–74) based on Jean Racine (1639–99)

*Joshua*, George Frederick Handel, text by Rev. T. Morell

*Lazarus* (or *The Feast of the Resurrection*), Franz Schubert (1797–1828)

*Samson*, George Frederick Handel, with poems by John Milton (1563–1647)

*St John Passion*, Johann Sebastian Bach (1685–1750), text from St John's Gospel

*St Matthew Passion*, Johann Sebastian Bach (1685–1750) text mainly from St Matthew's Gospel

*The Messiah* (1742), George Frederick Handel. One of the most famous sections is the 'Hallelujah Chorus', during which audiences traditionally stand because King George II stood in reverence to God as it was sung.

### Negro spirituals

These were songs originally sung by African-American slaves and were made famous by people like Paul Le Roy Robeson (1898–1976). They include: 'Swing low sweet chariot,

coming for to carry me home'
(reminding us of Elijah's chariot) and
'He's got the whole world in his
hands'.

## Popular hymns

Thousands of hymns have been
written; Isaac Watts (1674–1748)
wrote over 600, Charles Wesley
(1707–88) wrote over 5,000 and
Fanny Crosby (1820–1915) wrote
over 6,000. Those written for the
Christian festivals include:

### Christmas: (Isaiah 7:10–17; Matthew 2:1–12; Luke 2:1–20)

*Angels from the realms of glory*, James
 Montgomery (1771–1854)
*As with gladness men of old*, W. C. Dix
 (1837–98)
*Away in a manger, no crib for a bed*,
 originally by Martin Luther
 (1483–1546)
*Christians, awake, salute the happy
 morn*, John Byrom (1692–1763)
*Hark! the herald-angels sing*, Charles
 Wesley (1707–88)
*Infant holy, infant lowly*, Christina
 Rossetti (1830–94)
*O come, all ye faithful*, 17th-century
 Latin carol
*O little town of Bethlehem*, Phillips
 Brooks (1835–93)
*Once in royal David's city*, Cecil
 Frances Alexander (1818–95)
*While shepherds watched their flocks by
 night*, Nahum Tate (1652–1715)

### Easter (Isaiah 53; Matthew 28:1–20; Luke 24)

*And can it be that I should gain*,
 Charles Wesley (1707–88)
*'Man of sorrows' wondrous name*,
 Philip Bliss (1838–76)
*It is a thing most wonderful*, W.W.
 How (1823–97)
*There is a green hill far away*, Cecil
 Frances Alexander (1818–95)
*When I survey the wondrous cross*, Isaac
 Watts (1674–1748)
*Christ is risen, hallelujah!*, J.S.B.
 Monsell (1811–75)
*Christ the Lord is risen today!
 Hallelujah!*, Charles Wesley
 (1707–88)
*Low in the grave He lay*, Robert Lowry
 (1826–99)
*Thine be the glory, risen, conquering
 Son*, Edmond Budry (1854–1932)
*The head that once was crowned with
 thorns*, Thomas Kelly
 (1769–1855)

### Pentecost (Isaiah 32:15; Acts 2)

*Breathe on me breath of God*, Edwin
 Hatch (1835–89)
*Come down, O Love divine*, Bianco da
 Siena (c. 1350–1434)
*Come, Holy Ghost, our hearts inspire*,
 Charles Wesley (1707–88)
*Holy Spirit, truth divine*, Samuel
 Longfellow (1819–92)
*Spirit divine, attend our prayers*,
 Andrew Reed (1787–1862)

**Harvest (Psalm 65:9–13)**

*All things bright and beautiful*, Cecil
  Frances Alexander (1818–95)
*Come, ye thankful people, come*, Henry
  Alford (1810–71)
*For the beauty of the earth*, F.S.
  Pierpoint (1835–1917)
*O Lord of heaven and earth and sea*,
  Christopher Wordsworth
  (1807–85)
*Sing to the Lord of harvest*, J.S.B.
  Monsell (1811–75)
*We plough the fields and scatter*,
  Matthias Claudius (1740–1815)
*Yes, God is good; in earth and sky*, E.L.
  Follen and J.H. Gurney

## Modern 20th-century songs

These are often played by a musical
group or guitarist and include:
*As the deer pants for the water*, Martin
  Nystrom (Psalm 42:1)
*Father God I wonder*, Ian Smale
  (2 Thessalonians 2:16)
*Father I place into your hands,* Jenny
  Hewer (2 Corinthians 1:3)
*Holy Spirit we welcome you*, Chris A.
  Bowater (Acts 10:44)
*In your presence, I am content*, Chris A.
  Bowater (Psalm 131:2)
*Jesus put this song into our hearts*,
  Graham Kendrick (Psalm 40:3)
*Led like a lamb to the slaughter*,
  Graham Kendrick (Isaiah 53:7)
*Let there be love shared among us*, Dave
  Bilbrough (1 Thessalonians 2:8)

*Let your living water flow over my soul*,
  John Watson (John 7:38)
*Lord the light of your love is shining*,
  Graham Kendrick (John 1:4–5,9)
*Majesty, worship His majesty*, Jack
  Hayford (Micah 5:4)
*May the fragrance*, Graham Kendrick
  (2 Corinthians 2:14)
*Reign in Me*, Chris A Bowater
  (Matthew 6:10)
*To be in your presence*, Noel Richards
  (Psalm 16:11)
*We are here to praise you*, Graham
  Kendrick (Psalm 29:1)

## Musicals

The following have played to packed
theatres:
*Jesus Christ Superstar*, composed by
Andrew Lloyd Webber (1948–  )
*Joseph and his Amazing Technicolor*

## Musical instruments

Musical instruments mentioned in
the Bible include:

| | |
|---|---|
| Cymbals | 1 Chronicles 26:5 |
| Drum | Isaiah 24:8 |
| Harp | Psalm 147:7 |
| Horn | Psalm 98:6 |
| Flute | Genesis 4:21 |
| Lyre | Psalm 108:2 |
| Oboe | Daniel 3:15 |
| Rattles | 2 Samuel 6:5 |
| Tambourine | Exodus 15:20 |
| Trumpet | Joshua 6:4 |
| Zither | Daniel 3:5 |

*Dreamcoat*, composed by Andrew Lloyd Webber (1948– ).

# Poetry

## We are God's poem

Our word *poem* comes from the Greek word *poiēma* and is used in Ephesians 2:10. 'God has made us what we are [*poiēma*], and in our union with Christ Jesus he has created us for a life of good deeds, which he has already prepared for us to do.' So Christians are God's poem. Much poetry has been inspired by the Bible, including that in the following A–Z list of poets:

Addison, Joseph (1672–1719), *Ode* – Genesis 1:14–19

Brooke, Rupert (1887–1915), *Mary and Gabriel* – Luke 1:38

Cowper, William (1731–1800), *Sardis* – Revelation 3:1

Dickinson, Emily (1830–86), *A little east of Jordan* – Genesis 32:11–19

East, James T. (1860–1937), *Wise men seeking Jesus* – Matthew 2:1–12

Flint, Annie Johnson, *He giveth more* – James 4:6, Isaiah 40:29, Jude 2

Guyon, Jeanne (1648–1717) *A little bird am I* – Psalm 16:5

Herbert, George (1593–1633). *The Altar* – Deuteronomy 27:2–3

Ingelow, Jean (1820–97), *And didst Thou love the race that loved not Thee?* – Hebrews 9:24

Joyce, James (1882–1941), *My Dove, My Beautiful One* – Song of Songs 5:2

Keble, John (1792–1866), *Reason and Faith at once set out* – John 20:14–16

Longfellow, Henry Wadsworth (1807–82), *Blind Bartimaeus* – Mark 10:46

Milton, John (1608–74), *Paradise Lost* – Genesis

Newton, John (1725–1807), *How bitter that cup* – Matthew 27:46

Owen, Wilfred (1893–1918), *At a Calvary Near the Ancre* – John 15:12

Palgrave, Francis (1824–97), *Not throned above the skies* – Matthew 18:20

Quarles, Francis (1592–1644), *The generous Christian must as well improve* – Matthew 10:16

Rossetti, Christina Georgina (1830–89), *Eve* – Genesis 3:6

Scott, Sir Walter (1771–1832), *The Book of Books* – Genesis – Revelation

Tennyson, Alfred Lord (1809–1892), *In Memoriam* – John 1:1

Ufford, Edward Smith, *Throw out the Lifeline* – Romans 15:1

Very, Jones (1813–80), *Take ye Heed, Watch and Pray* – Mark 13:33

Wrintmore, F.W. (1903–78) *The Master* – Isaiah 61:1

Xavier, Francis (1506–52), *Thou O my Jesus* – Matthew 27:32–34

## Revelation

The soft blue sky reveals the Lord
  Who by His mighty power,
Upholds the kingdoms of the world,
  Through each momentous hour.

The golden hues of waving corn,
  Display His loveliness:
And raging seas declare His strength,
  And man's own nothingness.

The Cross of Christ unfolds a grace
  That cannot be denied:
A spaceless love embracing all,
  Great virtues unified.

My own poor heart reveals my need,
  A hunger for the Word
That comes as food to feed my soul,
  The manna of my Lord.

**F. H. Wrintmore (1903–78) (Matthew 4:4; Hebrews 4:12)**

Young, Andrew John (1885–1971), *There is a happy land* – Revelation 21:4

Zinzendorf, Nicolaus von (1700–60), *My Glorious Dress* – Revelation 7:9

# Art

## Engravings and etchings including:

*The sacrifice of Isaac* (Genesis 22:1), Rembrandt van Rijn (1606–69)

*The Prodigal Son* (Luke 15:11), Rembrandt van Rijn (1606–69)

*The Good Samaritan* (Luke 10:30), Julius Schnorr von Carolsfield (1794–1872)

*Peter sinking through lack of faith* (Matthew 14:30), Julius Schnorr von Carolsfield (1794–1872)

*Book of Revelation* (Revelation), Albrecht Dürer (1471–1528)

## Frescoes including:

*The Creation of the Sun and Moon* (Genesis 1:16)

*The Deluge* (Genesis 7:1)

*The Conversion of St Paul* (Acts 9:3)

*The Last Judgment* (Revelation 20)

These are some of the most famous and are all by Michelangelo Buonarroti (1475–1564) in the Sistine and Pauline Chapels at the Vatican.

*Mary's visit to Elizabeth* (Luke 1:39), The Church of the Visitation, Ein Karem, Israel

*The birth of Jesus* (Luke 2:7) and *Angels tell the shepherds of Jesus' birth* (Luke 2:8), The Shepherds' Field Church, Bethlehem

*Mary and Martha* (Luke 10:38) and *Lazarus rising from the dead* (John

11:43), The Church of Lazarus, Bethany

*The Transfiguration* (Luke 9:29), Basilica of the Transfiguration, Mt Tabor

*Life of St Paul* (2 Corinthans 11:22) by James Thornhill on dome of St Paul's Cathedral, London

## Illustrated manuscripts including:

*Lindisfarne Gospels*, named after the Northumbrian island monastery where the manuscripts were produced in the 7th century, probably by Eadfrith, Bishop of Lindisfarne in honour of St Cuthbert. They are now in the British Museum.

*Book of Hours* – these were books of devotions following the canonical hours i.e., matins, prime, tierce, sext, nones, vespers and compline, which were lavishly illuminated in the Middle Ages.

*Book of Kells* (8th-century) – the Gospels in Latin outstandingly illustrated. It is kept in the Library of Trinity College, Dublin.

## Mosaics including:

Byzantine mosaics of many biblical scenes, including Jesus; Adam and Eve (Genesis 2:22), Kariye Museum, Istanbul, Turkey

Loaves and fishes (Mark 6:30–44), at

# The Bible Code

Is there a code in the Bible which only the use of computers in this century has revealed? So says Eli Rips, world renowned Jewish mathematician. It is claimed this code reveals worldwide events. Sir Isaac Newton was certain there was a hidden code in the Bible, he learned Hebrew and spent half his life trying to find it. Sceptical mathematicians in America have tested Eli Rips' theory and confirmed that the theory is proved mathematically. Michael Drosnin in his book has done much research and shows how it works. The original Hebrew text was written in one long string (no sentences, verses, chapters, etc). He fed this into the computer and did 'skip sequences'. If the skip is 100 letters then the text forms a 'page' 100 letters wide. The result is a kind of crossword puzzle. Starting with the original word, giving the skip sequence, other connecting words can be found alongside, through or near the starting word as in a crossword puzzle. As an example, he claims that the words *Yitzhak Rabin, assassin who will assassinate* and *Amir* (the assassin's name) appear together. At present mathematicians have not been able to prove the theory wrong – maybe only time will tell.

the Church of the Multiplication, Tabgha, near Capernaum, Israel

Jesus (Revelation 5:9), at the Basilica of Hagia Sophia, Istanbul, Turkey

John the Baptist (Luke 3:7), at the Basilica of Hagia Sophia, Istanbul, Turkey

Mary and Child (Luke 2:16), on the apse of the Basilica of the Dormition, Mount Zion, Israel

Symbols of the Trinity and the apostles (Matthew 2:10), the Basilica of the Dormition, Mount Zion, Israel

The Virgin Mary (Luke 1:38), at the Basilica of Hagia Sophia, Istanbul, Turkey

## Paintings on canvas including:

*Elohim creating Adam* (Genesis 2:7), William Blake (1757–1827)

*Cain slaying Abel* (Genesis 4:8), Peter Paul Rubens (1577–1640)

*The angel preventing Abraham from sacrificing Isaac* (Genesis 22:10–12), Rembrandt van Rijn (1606–69)

*Isaac blessing Jacob* (Genesis 27:26–29), Bartolomé Esteban Murillo (1618–82)

*Moses in the bulrush basket* (Exodus 2:5), William Blake (1757–1827)

*Moses dividing the waters of the Red Sea* (Exodus 14:21–22), John Martin (1789–1854)

*The Scapegoat* (Leviticus 16:20–22), William Holman Hunt

(1827–1910)

*The adoration of the shepherds* (Luke 2:15–16), Sandro Botticelli (c. 1445–1510)

*Finding the Saviour in the Temple* (Luke 2:46), William Holman Hunt (1827–1910)

*Christ in the house of Martha and Mary* (Luke 10:38), Jan Vermeer (1632–75)

*The Prodigal Son* (Luke 15:11), Albrecht Dürer (1471–1528)

*The Good Samaritan* (Luke 10:30), Vincent van Gogh (1853–90)

*Christ stills the storm* (Mark 4:37), John Martin (1789–1854)

*Christ driving the traders from the Temple* (John 2:13), El Greco (1541–1610)

*The Last Supper* (Matthew 26:26), Leonardo da Vinci (1452–1519)

*Betrayal of Christ* (Mark 14:43), Anthony van Dyck (1599–1641)

*Crucifixion* (John 19:16), Peter Paul Rubens (1577–1640)

*The Supper at Emmaus* (Luke 24:28–31), Michelangelo Merisi da Caravaggio (1573–1610)

*The Light of the World* (Revelation 3:20), William Holman Hunt (1827–1910)

## Sculptures including:

*Moses* (Deuteronomy 34:10), for the tomb of Pope Julius III, Michelangelo (1475–1564)

*David, holding the stone which slew*

*Goliath* (1 Samuel 17:49), Michelangelo (1475–1564) in Florence

*Madonna and child* (Matthew 2:11), Henry Moore (1898–1986) in St Matthews, Northampton

*Pietà* (pity), St Mary the Virgin mourning over Jesus (John 19:26), Michelangelo (1475–1564), St Peter's Basilica, Vatican

*St Michael victorious over the dragon* (Revelation 12:7–8), Jacob Epstein (1880–1959) at Coventry Cathedral

*Christ the Redeemer*, statue (1 Timothy 2:5-6), standing 100ft (30 mtrs) high on Corcovado (the hunchback mountain), overlooking Rio de Janeiro, Brazil, created by a team of sculptors headed by French sculptor Paul Landowsky

## Stained-glass windows including:

*The Chagall Windows*, depicting the twelve tribes of Israel (Numbers 26:5) by Marc Chagall (1887–1985), at the Synagogue of the Hadassah, Hebrew University Medical Centre, Jerusalem

*The Menorah* (Exodus 25:31–40), at Hechal Sholomo, the seat of the Chief Rabbinate of Israel, Jerusalem

*Aaron the High Priest* (Leviticus 6:22), in Chartres Cathedral, France

Biblical scenes which appear in the stained-glass windows of churches and cathedrals all around Britain

*Creation* (Genesis 1), Edward Burne Jones (1833–98), at Waltham Abbey, Essex

*Nativity* (Luke 2:7), Edward Burne Jones (1833–98), at Jesus College, Cambridge

*John the Baptist* (John 1:6), Edward Burne Jones (1833–98)

*Crucifixion* (Matthew 27:35), Brian Thomas, east window in St Paul's Cathedral, London

*The Ascension* (Acts 1:9–11), Le Mans Cathedral, France

*The last judgment* (Revelation 20:13), Edward Burne Jones (1833-98), at Birmingham Cathedral

## Wood carvings including:

*Apostles* (Matthew 10:2), carved on the porch of Malmesbury Abbey

*The Penitent Magdalene* (Luke 8:2), Donatello (Donato di Betto Bardi) (c.1386–1466)

*John the Baptist* (Matthew 21:32), Donatello (c.1386–1466)

*Paul* (Galatians 1:1), *Matthew and Thomas* (Mark 3:18), Nicolas de Haguengeau (1445–1526)

# So you think you know your Bible?

## Bible quizzes

The answers to the quizzes are at the end of the chapter.

## First things first

1. Where did Jesus perform his first miracle?
2. Who was the first Christian martyr?
3. Which was the first creature to leave the ark?
4. Who was the first murderer?

5. Who was the first judge of Israel?
6. Who was the first hunter?
7. What is the first commandment with a promise?
8. Where were the disciples first called Christians?
9. Who was the first king of Israel?
10. Where is the first occurrence of the phrase, 'put his trust in the Lord'?

## Who's who?

1. What were the names of Daniel's companions who were thrown into the fiery furnace?
2. What was the name of John the Baptist's father?
3. What was the name of Samuel's mother?
4. What was the name of the 'dealer in purple cloth' at Philippi?
5. What was the name of the old prophetess in the temple when Mary and Joseph presented the baby Jesus to God?

# All Change

Saul became Paul; what were the original names of these Bible Characters?

1. Abraham
2. Belteshazzar
3. Cephas or Peter
4. Joshua
5. Marah

6. What was the name of the youngest son of Jacob and Rachel?
7. Who is the youngest king mentioned in the Bible?
8. What was the name of the slave who ran away from Philemon?
9. Who was Ruth's mother-in-law?
10. Who was Paul's teacher and a member of the Council?
11. What was the name of the silversmith at Ephesus who made souvenirs at the temple of Diana (Artemis)?
12. Which Jewish girl became queen of Persia?

13. Can you name two of Aaron's four children?
14. What was the name of Pharaoh's official in whose household Joseph served?
15. What was the name of Barnabas' cousin who was Paul's co-worker for a time?

# Well-known and not so well-known women

Can you identify the following?

1. Abigail
2. Zipporah
3. Tabitha (Dorcas)
4. Joanna
5. Syntyche
6. Priscilla
7. Michal
8. Jezebel
9. Eunice
10. Leah

# Well-known and not so well-known men

Can you identify the following?

1. Caleb
2. Uriah
3. Zophar
4. Zenas
5. Nicodemus

6. Archippus
7. Methuselah
8. Chuza
9. Pekah
10. Japheth

# Who said it?

Who spoke the following words?
1. 'You will know the truth, and the truth will set you free.'
2. 'Speak, your servant is listening.'
3. 'My name is Mob.'
4. 'May the LORD bless you and take care of you; May the LORD be kind and gracious to you; May the LORD look on you with favour and give you peace.'
5. 'What is truth?'
6. 'We do not know what to do, but we look to you for help.'
7. 'Wherever you go, I will go; wherever you live, I will live. Your people will be my people, and your God will be my God.'
8. 'What must I do to be saved?'
9. 'Yet who knows – maybe it was for a time like this that you were made queen!'
10. 'You are that man!'
11. 'Can these bones come back to life?'
12. 'Bring the full amount of your tithes to the Temple, so that there will be plenty of food there.'
13. 'I am not good enough even to carry his sandals.'
14. 'I have been given all authority in heaven and on earth. Go, then, to all peoples everywhere and make them my disciples: baptize them in the name of the Father, the Son, and the Holy Spirit, and teach them to obey everything I have commanded you. And I will be with you always, to the end of the age.'
15. 'Has Saul become a prophet?'
16. 'Everything is a gift from you, and we have only given back what is yours already.'
17. 'Where is the baby born to be the king of the Jews? … we have come to worship him.'
18. 'The spirit is willing, but the flesh is weak.'
19. 'In this short time do you think you will make me a Christian?'
20. 'Wasn't it like a fire burning in us when he talked to us on the road and explained the Scriptures to us?'

# Occupations of people in the Bible

1. What were the occupations of Simon Peter and Andrew?
2. In the Acts of the Apostles, what was the occupation of Cornelius?
3. To whom did God give 'skill, ability, and understanding for every kind of artistic work'?
4. The apostle Paul, Aquila and Priscilla were all …?

5. What was the occupation of Luke?

6. What was the name of Rebekah's nurse?

7. Fill in the missing word: '..., obey your earthly masters in everything.'

8. What was the occupation of Simon, who lived in Joppa?

9. In Paul's letter to Titus, he mentions Zenas – what was Zenas' occupation?

10. In the book of Ezra, what was the occupation of Mithredath?

11. What was the occupation of Joseph, Jesus' father?

12. What was the occupation of the prophet Amos?

13. What occupation is the law likened to in Paul's letter to the Galatians?

14. Who was described as 'a great hunter'?

15. Uzziel helped repair Jerusalem's walls; what was his real occupation?

16. What were the occupations of Cain and Abel?

17. Zacchaeus and Matthew (Levi) were both .........?

18. Who is the first smith mentioned in the Bible?

19. In 2 Timothy, Paul comments on a man named Alexander. What was Alexander's job?

20. What was Nehemiah's occupation?

# Death ... and resurrection

1. Who raised Tabitha (Dorcas) from the dead?

2. Which king killed himself by falling on his own sword?

3. Fill in the missing words: 'For sin pays its wage – ......; but God's free gift is ...... ...... in union with Christ Jesus our Lord.'

4. Who was killed for touching the ark of the covenant?

5. According to Matthew's Gospel, who rolled back the stone from Jesus' tomb?

6. To whom did Jesus say these words: 'I am the resurrection and the life. Those who believe in me will live, even though they die; and all those who live and believe in me will never die.' Do you believe this?

7. 185,000 of which nation were put to death by the angel of the LORD?

8. Which king who was ill and at the point of death was given an additional 15 years of life?

9. Which married couple fell down dead after it was revealed that they had lied about the price of the piece of property which they had sold?

10. Who buried Abraham?

11. To whom did Jesus say, 'I promise you that today you will be in Paradise with me'?

12. Which book and chapter of the Bible does this quotation come from:

'I passed on to you what I received, which is of the greatest importance: that Christ died for our sins, as written in the Scriptures; that he was buried and that he was raised to life three days later, as written in the Scriptures; that he appeared to Peter and then to all twelve apostles. Then he appeared to more than 500 of his followers at once … Then he appeared to James, and afterwards to all the apostles. Last of all he appeared also to me – even though I am like someone whose birth was abnormal.'

# Animals of the Bible

1. What kind of animal, belonging to Balaam, spoke God's words?

2. According to Jesus, it is easier for which animal to go through the eye of a needle than for a rich man to enter the kingdom of God?

3. Which animals, according to prophecy, would devour Jezebel's flesh?

4. Who gained experience by fighting off lions and bears from sheep?

5. Fill in the name of the missing creature in this quotation: 'Like …… that dissolve into slime; may they be like a baby born dead that never sees the light.'

6. In the book of Joel, which creature is used as a warning of God's judgement?

7. In one of the psalms, the writer compares an animal's thirst for water with his own longing for God. Which animal is used in the comparison?

8. Which two Philistine animals were used to carry the ark of the covenant back to Israel?

9. What creatures were given out at the feeding of the 5,000?

10. The death of Herod is said to be caused by his being eaten by which creatures?

11. Upon which animal did Jesus ride into Jerusalem?

12. Jesus advised against throwing pearls to which animals?

13. When Moses threw his staff on the ground, which creature did it turn into?

14. Which animal did Jesus liken false prophets to?

15. In what creature did Peter find a four-drachma coin?

16. When some youths jeered at Elisha for being bald, which animals came and mauled the youths?

17. Which four kinds of creatures were sent as plagues upon Egypt?

18. Into which animals did Jesus send the legion of evil spirits that he had cast out of a man?

19. In the Song of Solomon (Song of Songs), the lover likens the beloved's breasts to which animals?

20. Job 40:15–24 describes a great beast, the behemoth. Which animal is this identifed as?

21. Fill in the name of the missing creature: 'Lazy people should learn a lesson from the way ...... live.'

22. Fill in the name of the missing animal: '......: they are not strong either, but they make their homes among the rocks.'

23. Job 41:1–34 describes a large marine animal, the leviathan. Which animal is this identified as?

24. In the rules about clean and unclean food, which kind of land animals could not be eaten?

25. An effigy of which animal did Moses put on a pole, so that anyone who had been bitten by this animal could look at it and live?

## Birds of the Bible

1. Jesus said that Peter would disown him three times before he heard the sound of which bird?

2. Jesus compared the concern that he felt for Jerusalem to what?

3. Where there is a carcass, which birds gather?

4. David described himself as being abandoned like which bird in the ruins?

5. In which parable do birds play a significant role?

6. What birds did Joseph and Mary bring as a sacrifice when they presented Jesus in the temple?

7. Who had a vision of a lion with the wings of an eagle?

8. Fill in the name of the missing creature: 'Those who trust in the LORD for help will find their strength renewed. They will rise on wings like ......; they will run and not get weary; they will walk and not grow weak.'

9. Which bird, according to the psalmist, makes its nest in the pine trees?

10. Which bird fed Elijah?

11. At Jesus' baptism, the Spirit of God descended on Jesus in the form of which kind of bird?

12. Which bird did the Israelites feed on as they journeyed from Egypt?

13. According to the book of Proverbs, what is an undeserved curse like?

14. According to the book of Job, which bird treats its young harshly?

15. Jesus said to his disciples, 'Do not be afraid; you are worth much more than many ......'

# Plants of the Bible

1. What kind of branches did the crowd take to welcome Jesus as he made his triumphal entry into Jerusalem?

2. What was more beautiful than Solomon in all his splendour?

3. What kind of tree did Zacchaeus climb to see Jesus?

4. What kind of wood was the ark of the covenent made of?

5. On which plant was a sponge of wine vinegar lifted to Jesus' lips as he was on the cross?

6. Rachel and Leah argued over which herb?

7. Which fruit was used as a decorative model on the pillars in Solomon's temple?

8. Complete the following: 'The righteous will flourish like ...... trees, they will grow like the ...... of Lebanon.'

9. Which spices did the teachers of the law and Pharisees give a tenth of?

10. Which tree did Jesus curse?

11. Aaron's staff, placed before the LORD in the Tent of Testimony, sprouted, budded, blossomed and produced what?

12. One of the gifts the Magi brought to Jesus was gold. What were the other two?

13. What did the Old Testament grain offering consist of?

14. Jesus called himself the real ......, to which all his disciples are joined.

15. From which tree did the wood come with which Solomon made harps and lyres?

16. Which spices did Nicodemus bring to wrap Jesus' body in?

17. Which tree and seed did Jesus use to illustrate and explain faith and the kingdom of God?

18. Complete the following quotation: 'Some of the branches of the cultivated ...... tree have been broken off, and a branch of a wild ...... tree has been joined to it. You Gentiles are like that wild ...... tree.'

19. Which kinds of grain did not suffer from the plague of hail because they were ripened at a later time?

20. Under the stalks of which plant did Rahab hide the spies?

# Dreamers of dreams

1. In the words of one Old Testament prophet, there would come a time when 'old people will have dreams'. Who was the prophet?

2. In the Old Testament, which three Egyptians did Joseph interpret dreams for?

3. Matthew records five dreams in connection with Jesus' birth and infancy. In how many of them does an angel appear?

4. To whom did the LORD appear in a dream, saying, 'What would you like me to give you'?

5. In Nebuchadnezzar's dream of a statue, what was it that struck the statue?

6. In Daniel's interpretation of Nebuchadnezzar's dream of a tree, who is represented by the large strong tree that is cut down?

7. In which Bible book do these words occur: 'I know what those prophets have said who speak lies in my name and claim that I have given them my messages in their dreams.'

8. Who said, 'In a dream last night I suffered much on account of him [Jesus]'?

# Colours of the Bible

1. What colour did Jesus' clothes become in the Transfiguration?

2. What colour was the cloth which Lydia dealt in?

3. What colour skies did Jesus use to comment on the weather?

4. What was the colour of the grass at the feeding of the 5,000?

5. What colours were Mordecai's royal garments?

6. Fill in the colours: 'You are stained …… with sin, but I will wash you as clean as snow. Although your stains are deep ……, you will be as …… as wool.'

7. What colour robe did the soldiers put on Jesus before they mocked him?

# ... who shall be nameless

The names of the people in the following questions are not recorded in the Bible, although their actions are.

1. Which of Paul's relations saved Paul's life?
2. Which woman, whose son Elisha raised from the dead, made her home available to Elisha?
3. To whose mother did the angel of the Lord appear to say that she would bear a son who was to be a Nazirite?
4. Which person, whose giving has become proverbially well-known, put all she had into the temple treasury?
5. Who looked back ... and became a pillar of salt?
6. Who had been married five times?
7. Who said of Jesus, 'He really was the Son of God'?

8. What is the colour of hair of an unclean person with a sore on the head or chin?
9. What colours are the hairs of old age?
10. What colour was Joseph's cup that was put into Benjamin's sack?

# Famous first words

Which Bible book begins ...

1. 'In the beginning the Word already existed; the Word was with God, and the Word was God.'
2. 'From Paul, a servant of Christ Jesus and an apostle chosen and called by God to preach his Good News.'
3. 'How lonely lies Jerusalem, once so full of people! Once honoured by the world, she is now like a widow; the noblest of cities has fallen into slavery.'
4. 'Happy are those who reject the advice of evil people, who do not follow the example of sinners or join those who have no use for God.'
5. 'Long ago, in the days before Israel had a king, there was a famine in the land. So a man named Elimelech ... went with his wife Naomi and their two sons Mahlon and Chilion to live for a while in the country of Moab.'
6. 'Dear Theophilus: In my first book I wrote about all the things that Jesus did and taught ...'
7. 'From the Elder – To my dear Gaius, whom I truly love.'
8. 'In the past, God spoke to our ancestors many times and in many ways through the prophets.'
9. 'In the beginning, when God created the universe ...'
10. 'On the fifth day of the fourth month of the thirtieth year, I ... was living with the Jewish exiles ... The

sky opened, and I saw a vision of God.'

11. 'This is the Good News about Jesus Christ, the Son of God.'

12. 'After the death of the LORD's servant Moses, the LORD spoke ...'

# The last word

Which Bible book ends ...

1. 'There was no king in Israel at that time. All the people did just as they pleased.'

2. 'But continue to grow in the grace and knowledge of our Lord and Saviour Jesus Christ. To him be the glory, now and for ever! Amen.'

3. 'David: Perez, Hezron, Ram, Amminadab, Nahshon, Salmon, Boaz, Obed, Jesse, David.'

4. 'He will bring fathers and children together again; otherwise I would have to come and destroy your country.'

5. 'And you, ... be faithful to the end. Then you will die, but you will rise to receive your reward at the end of time.'

6. 'Now, there are many other things that Jesus did. If they were all written down one by one, I suppose that the whole world could not hold the books that would be written.'

7. 'Give her credit for all she does. She deserves the respect of everyone.'

8. 'No other prophet has been able to do the great and terrifying things that Moses did in the sight of all Israel.'

9. 'As they leave, they will see the dead bodies of those who have rebelled against me. The worms that eat them will never die, and the fire that burns them will never be put out. The sight of them will be disgusting to the whole human race.'

10. 'The grace of the Lord Jesus Christ, the love of God, and the fellowship of the Holy Spirit be with you all.'

11. 'Remember all this, O God, and give me credit for it.'

12. '... to the only God our Saviour, through Jesus Christ our Lord, be glory, majesty, might, and authority, from all ages past, and now, and for ever and ever! Amen.'

# But God ...

Can you identify the settings (or at least the books of the Bible) in which the following 'but' – quotations occur?

1. 'You plotted evil against me, *but* God turned it into good ...'

2. 'They look at the outward appearance, *but* I [the LORD] look at the heart.'

3. '*But* because of our sins he was wounded, beaten because of the evil we did.'

4. 'I sowed the seed, Apollos watered the plant, *but* it was God who made the plant grow.'

5. 'God has overlooked the times when people did not know him, *but*

now he commands all of them everywhere to turn away from their evil ways.'

6. '*But* now God's way of putting people right with himself has been revealed.'

7. 'For sin pays its wage – death; *but* God's free gift is eternal life in union with Christ Jesus our Lord.

8. 'This means that death is at work in us, *but* life is at work in you.'

9. '*But* the truth is that Christ has been raised from death, as the guarantee that those who sleep in death will also be raised.'

10. 'Three times I prayed to the Lord about this and asked him to take it away. *But* his answer was: "My grace is all you need, for my power is greatest when you are weak."'

11. '*But* when the right time finally came, God sent his own Son. He came as the son of a human mother and lived under the Jewish Law, to redeem those who were under the Law...'

12. '*But* God's mercy is so abundant, and his love for us is so great, that while we were spiritually dead in our disobedience he brought us to life with Christ. It is by God's grace that you have been saved.'

13. 'You were at one time spiritually dead because of your sins and because you were Gentiles without the Law. *But* God has now brought you to life with Christ. God forgave us all our sins.'

14. 'Every Jewish priest performs his services every day and offers the same sacrifices many times; *but* these sacrifices can never take away sins. Christ, however, offered one sacrifice for sins, an offering that is effective for ever, and then he sat down at the right-hand side of God.'

15. 'In the past, God spoke to our ancestors many times and in many ways through the prophets, *but* in these last days he has spoken to us through his Son. He is the one through whom God created the universe, the one whom God has chosen to possess all things at the end.

He reflects the brightness of God's glory and is the exact likeness of God's own being, sustaining the universe with his powerful word. After achieving forgiveness for human sins, he sat down in heaven at the right-hand side of God, the Supreme Power.'

# Bible landscapes

1. On which mountain range did Noah's boat come to rest after the flood?

2. On which mountain did Moses receive the ten commandments?

3. On which mountain did Aaron die?

4. On which mountain did Elijah meet the prophets of Baal?

5. 'Instead, you have come to Mount .......... and to the city of the living God, the heavenly Jerusalem, with its thousands of angels.'

6. On which mountain were the bodies of Saul and his two sons found?

7. On which mountain was the Temple built?

8. To which mountain did Jesus and the disciples go after the last supper?

9. Which valley did Lot choose for himself?

10. In which valley did David have memorable victories against the Edomites?

11. In which valley did Delilah live?

12. Through which sea did God make dry ground for the Israelites to pass?

13. In his vision, into which sea did Ezekiel see fresh water flow?

14. 'The victories of Israel became known to all the kings west of the Jordan – in the hills, in the foothills, and all along the coastal plain of the .......... Sea as far north as Lebanon'

15. Which cave did Abraham buy for a burial ground?

16. Beside which lake were Simon and Andrew catching fish when Jesus invited them to catch people?

17. Over which river did Jacob send his two wives, two concubines and eleven children before wrestling at Peniel?

18. Which river figured in the king of Egypt's dreams, which Joseph interpreted?

19. In which river did John the Baptist baptize?

20. 'Elijah obeyed the LORD's command, and went and stayed by the brook of ..........'

21. Which brook did Jesus and the disciples cross to get to the garden outside Jerusalem?

## Put it in writing

1. Which book of the Bible mentions 'the Lamb's book of the living'?

2. Which prophet ate a scroll and found it as sweet and honey?

3. In which city did new believers (formerly sorcerers) burn their scrolls publicly?

4. Which event is said to be described in the 'Book of Jashar'?

5. Who wrote 'When you come, bring my coat that I left in Troas with Carpus; bring the books too'?

# Chapter and verse

Can you give the exact book, chapter and verse of the following quotations? (If this is too difficult, just the name of the book will do!)

1. 'We know that in all things God works for good with those who love him, those whom he has called according to his purpose.'

2. 'Listen! I stand at the door and knock; if anyone hears my voice and opens the door, I will come in and eat with them, and they will eat with me.'

3. 'Would any of you who are fathers give your son a snake when he asks for fish?'

4. 'Go in through the narrow gate, because the gate to hell is wide and the road that leads to it is easy, and there are many who travel it. But the gate to life is narrow and the way that leads to it is hard, and there are few people who find it.'

5. 'No one can explain by himself or herself a prophecy in the Scriptures.'

6. 'Your eyes are too holy to look at evil, and you cannot stand the sight of people doing wrong.'

7. 'Anyone who is joined to Christ is a new being; the old is gone, the new has come.'

8. 'You will name him Jesus – because he will save his people from their sins.'

9. 'I pray that your love will keep on growing more and more, together with true knowledge and perfect judgement, so that you will be able to choose what is best ... Your lives will be filled with the truly good qualities which only Jesus Christ can produce, for the glory and praise of God.'

10. 'Fling wide the gates, open the ancient doors, and the great king will come in.'

11. 'Do two people start travelling together without arranging to meet?'

12. 'What we see now is like a dim image in a mirror; then we shall see face to face.'

13. 'Even the weak must fight.'

14. 'I can see people, but they look like trees walking about.'

15. 'God said, "Do not come any closer. Take off your sandals, because you are standing on holy ground."'

16. 'The Lord has told us what is good. What he requires of us is this: to do what is just, to show constant love, and to live in humble fellowship with our God.'

17. 'Fools say to themselves, "There is no God."'

18. 'Trust in the Lord with all your heart. Never rely on what you think you know. Remember the Lord in everything you do, and he will show you the right way.'

19. 'Take the teachings that you heard me proclaim in the presence of many witnesses, and entrust them to reliable people, who will be able to teach others also.'

20. 'After the seven months are over, men will be chosen to travel through

the land in order to find and bury those bodies remaining on the ground, so that they can make the land clean.'

21. 'What are the angels, then? They are spirits who serve God and are sent by him to help those who are to receive salvation.'

22. 'The LORD gave, and now he has taken away. May his name be praised!'

23. '[Jesus] at once got into a boat with his disciples and went to the district of Dalmanutha.'

24. 'You know that I did not hold back anything that would be of help to you as I preached and taught in public and in your homes.'

## As it is written …

The following Old Testament quotations are quoted in full or in part in the New Testament. Can you name the book (with chapter and verse reference, if possible) in which they originally occur in the Old Testament?

1. 'A young woman who is pregnant will have a son and will name him "Immanuel".'

2. 'Human beings must not depend on bread alone to sustain them, but on everything that the LORD says.'

3. 'Eye for eye, tooth for tooth.'

4. 'So they paid me 30 pieces of silver as my wages.'

5. 'I will be with you; I will be your

## How's your spelling?

Which is the correct spelling of the following names of books of the Bible?

1. a) Habbakuk b) Habakkuk c) Habakuk
2. a) Phillipians b) Philipians c) Philippians
3. a) Zechariah b) Zachariah c) Zacharias
4. a) Ecclesiastes b) Eclesiastes c) Eclessiastes
5. a) Isiah b) Isaiah c) Isiaih

God, and you will be my people.'

6. 'Rejoice, rejoice, people of Zion! Shout for joy, you people of Jerusalem! Look, your king is coming to you! He comes triumphant and victorious, but humble and riding on a donkey – on a colt, the foal of a donkey.'

7. 'The LORD said to my lord, "Sit here at my right until I put your enemies under your feet."'

# 3:16's

The following verses all have 3:16 as their chapter and verse reference. Which books of the Bible do they come from?

1. 'For God loved the world so much that he gave his only Son, so that everyone who believes in him may not die but have eternal life.'
2. 'All Scripture is inspired by God and is useful for teaching the truth, rebuking error, correcting faults, and giving instruction for right living.'
3. 'Surely you know that you are God's temple and that God's Spirit lives in you!'
4. 'Then the people who feared the Lord spoke to one another, and the Lord listened and heard what they said. In his presence, there was written down in a book a record of those who feared the Lord and respected him.'
5. 'Christ's message in all its richness must live in your hearts. Teach and instruct each other with all wisdom. Sing psalms, hymns, and sacred songs; sing to God with thanksgiving in your hearts.'

8. 'Love your neighbour as you love yourself.'
9. 'I will send my messenger to prepare the way for me.'
10. 'He will send you a prophet like me from among your own people, and you are to obey him.'
11. 'How wonderful it is to see a messenger coming across the mountains, bringing good news, the news of peace! He announces victory and says to Zion, "Your God is king!"'
12. 'When Israel was a child, I loved him and called him out of Egypt as my son.'
13. 'A dead body hanging on a post brings God's curse on the land.'
14. 'The LORD says, "The time is coming when I will make a new covenant with the people of Israel and with the people of Judah. It will not be like the old covenant that I made with their ancestors when I took them by the hand and led them out of Egypt. Although I was like a husband to them, they did not keep that covenant. The new covenant that I will make with the people of Israel will be this: I will put my law within them and write it on their hearts. I will be their God, and they will be my people. None of them will have to teach his fellow-citizen to know the LORD, because all will know me, from the least to the greatest. I will forgive their sins and I will no longer

remember their wrongs. I, the LORD,
have spoken." '
15. 'If your enemies are hungry, feed
them; if they are thirsty, give them a
drink. You will make them burn with
shame, and the LORD will reward you.'

# Answers

## First things first

1. Cana in Galilee (John 2:1–11).
2. Stephen (Acts 6:8–8:2).
3. The raven (Genesis 8:7).
4. Cain (Genesis 4:8).
5. Othniel (Judges 3:9).
6. Nimrod (Genesis 10:9).
7. 'Respect your father and mother' (Exodus 20:12; Ephesians 6:2).
8. Antioch (Acts 11:26).
9. Saul (1 Samuel 9–10).
10. Genesis 15:6, describing Abram.

## Who's who?

1. Shadrach, Meshach and Abednego (Daniel 3).
2. Zechariah (Luke 1).
3. Hannah (1 Samuel 1–2).
4. Lydia (Acts 16:14).
5. Anna (Luke 2:36–38).
6. Benoni or Benjamin (Genesis 35:18).
7. Joash, who began his reign at the age of seven (2 Chronicles 24:1).
8. Onesimus (Philemon).
9. Naomi (Ruth 1:22).
10. Gamaliel (Acts 5:34; 22:3).
11. Demetrius (Acts 19:24).
12. Esther (Esther).

13. Nadab, Abihu, Eleazar, and Ithamar (Exodus 6:23).
14. Potiphar (Genesis 37:36; 39).
15. John Mark (Acts 12:12; 15:37–38; Colossians 4:10).

## All change

1. Abram (Genesis 17:5).
2. Daniel (Daniel 1:7).
3. Simon (John 1:42).
4. Hoshea (Numbers 13:16).
5. Naomi (Ruth 1:20).

## Well-known and not so well-known women

1. The wife of Nabal, who later became David's wife (1 Samuel 25:3–42).
2. The daughter of Reuel and wife of Moses (Exodus 2:21).
3. A woman noted for her good works; raised from the dead by Peter (Acts 9:36–43).
4. One of the women who provided for Jesus and the Twelve (Luke 8:3).
5. A woman in the church at Philippi who was having a disagreement with Euodia (Philippians 4:2).

6. The wife of Aquila; co-worker with Paul and instructor of Apollos (Acts 18).

7. A daughter of Saul and wife of David. She criticized David for dancing before the ark (1 Samuel 14:49; 18:27; 2 Samuel 6:16–23).

8. The wife of Ahab. She promoted Baal worship, killed prophets of the LORD and opposed Elijah (1 Kings 16–19).

9. The mother of Timothy (2 Timothy 1:5).

10. The elder daughter of Laban, Jacob's wife and mother of six of his sons (Genesis 29:16–33:7).

# Well-known and not so well-known men

1. One of those sent to spy out Canaan; he was allowed to enter the land because of his faith (Numbers 13–14; Joshua 14–15).

2. The Hittite husband of Bathsheba, sent to his death by David (2 Samuel 11).

3. One of Job's 'friends' (Job 2:11).

4. The lawyer mentioned in Titus 3:13.

5. The Pharisee who came to Jesus by night (John 3).

6. A Christian at Colosse and friend of Philemon (Colossians 4:17; Philemon 2).

7. The longest lived patriarch, who lived for 969 years (Genesis 5:22–27).

8. The manager of Herod's household; his wife Joanna and others supported the Twelve (Luke 8:3).

9. The son of Remaliah, and king of Israel (2 Kings 15:27).

10. One of Noah's sons (Genesis 9:18).

# Who said it?

1. Jesus speaking to the Jews who had believed him (John 8:32, GNB).

2. Samuel, to the LORD (1 Samuel 3:1–21; the quotation comes in verse 10, GNB).

3. The demon-possessed man of the Gerasenes (Gadarenes). Jesus cast out the demons into a herd of pigs, which rushed down a steep bank into the lake, where they drowned (Mark 5:1–20). The quotation is in verse 9.

4. The LORD telling Moses that he should tell Aaron and his sons to bless the Israelites in this way (Numbers 6:24–26, GNB).

5. Pilate speaking to Jesus at Jesus' 'trial' before Pilate (John 18:38).

6. King Jehoshaphat, at the conclusion of his prayer (2 Chronicles 20:12, GNB).

7. Ruth to Naomi (Ruth 1:16, NIV).

8. The Philippian jailer to Paul and Silas (Acts 16:30).

9. Mordecai to Esther, queen of Persia (Esther 4:14, GNB).

10. Nathan rebuking David, after David had caused the death of Uriah

the Hittite (2 Samuel 12:1–10, GNB; the quotation is in verse 7).

11. The LORD speaking to Ezekiel, after the Spirit of the LORD had brought him into the valley of dry bones (Ezekiel 37:1–3; the quotation comes in verse 3).

12. The LORD Almighty (Malachi 3:10, GNB).

13. John the Baptist, talking about Jesus (Matthew 3:11, GNB).

14. Jesus, speaking to the eleven disciples after his resurrection and before his ascension (Matthew 28:18–20), GNB; the 'Great Commission').

15. 'People who had known him [Saul] before', upon seeing Saul also prophesying among the prophets at Gibeah (1 Samuel 10:9–11, GNB; the quotation is in verse 11).

16. David, in his prayer of thanksgiving (1 Chronicles 29:1–19; the quotation comes in verse 14, GNB).

17. Men who studied the stars (traditionally known as the Wise Men) (Matthew 2:2, GNB).

18. Jesus to the sleeping disciples in Gethsemane (Matthew 26:41, GNB).

19. King Agrippa to Paul (Acts 26:28, GNB).

20. Two of Jesus' followers on the road to Emmaus (Luke 24:13–35; the quotation comes in verse 32, GNB).

# Occupations of people in the Bible

1. Fishermen (Matthew 4:18).

2. He was a captain in the Italian Regiment (Acts 10:1).

3. Bezalel (Exodus 35:30–31, GNB).

4. Tentmakers (Acts 18:1–3).

5. A doctor (Colossians 4:14).

6. Deborah (Genesis 35:8).

7. Slaves (Colossians 3:22, NIV).

8. A tanner (Acts 9:43; 10:6, 32).

9. A lawyer (Titus 3:13).

10. A treasurer (Ezra 1:8).

11. A carpenter (Matthew 13:55).

12. A shepherd (Amos 1:1).

13. A 'schoolmaster to bring us unto Christ' (Galatians 3:24, AV).

14. Nimrod (Genesis 10:9).

15. Goldsmith (Nehemiah 3:8).

16. They were farmers: 'Abel became a shepherd, but Cain was a farmer' (Genesis 4:2).

17. Tax collectors (Matthew 9:10–11; Luke 19:2).

18. Tubal Cain, a worker in metal (Genesis 4:22).

19. A metalworker (2 Timothy 4:14).

20. Wine steward to the king (Nehemiah 1:11).

# Death … and resurrection

1. Peter (Acts 9:36–43).

2. Saul (1 Samuel 31:4).

3. Death; eternal life (Romans 6:23, GNB).

4. Uzzah (2 Samuel 6:6–7).

5. An angel of the Lord (Matthew 28:2).

6. Martha, sister of Lazarus (John 11:25–26, GNB).

7. Assyria (2 Kings 19:35).

8. Hezekiah (2 Kings 20:1–11).

9. Ananias and Sapphira (Acts 5:1–11).

10. His sons Isaac and Ishmael (Genesis 25:9).

11. The penitent criminal who was crucified at the same time as Jesus (Luke 23:43).

12. 1 Corinthians 15 (verses 3–8).

# Animals of the Bible

1. A donkey (ass) (Numbers 22:21–41).

2. A camel (Matthew 19:24).

3. Dogs (1 Kings 21:23; 2 Kings 30:30–37).

4. David (1 Samuel 17:34–35).

5. Snail (Psalm 58:8, GNB).

6. The locust (e.g. Joel 1:4).

7. A deer (Psalm 42:1).

8. Two (milch) cows that had calved and had never been yoked (1 Samuel 6:7).

9. Two fish (together with five loaves of bread) (Matthew 14:13–21).

10. Worms (Acts 12:23). 'His death is not regarded as accidental, but as a judgement arising from his pride and

his aspiration to divine status' (*The New International Dictionary of the Bible*).

11. A colt (Matthew 21:1–11).

12. Pigs (swine) (Matthew 7:6).

13. A snake (Exodus 4:1–4).

14. Those who 'are really like wild wolves' but who come in sheep's clothing (Matthew 7:15).

15. A fish (Matthew 17:27).

16. Two bears (2 Kings 2:23–25).

17. Frogs, gnats, flies and locusts (Exodus 8–10).

18. A herd of pigs (swine) (Mark 5:1–17).

19. 'Your breasts are like gazelles, twin deer feeding among lilies' (Song of Songs 4:5, GNB).

20. 'Possibly the hippopotamus or elephant' (GNB footnote).

21. Ant (Proverbs 6:6, GNB).

22. Rock-badgers, that is the hyrax or coney (Proverbs 30:26).

23. 'Possibly the crocodile' (GNB footnote).

24. Those that chew the cud (ruminants) or have a split hoof (Leviticus 11:1–8; Deuteronomy 14:3–8).

25. A bronze snake (Numbers 21:4–9; see also John 3:14–15).

# Birds of the Bible

1. Before the cock crows (Matthew 26:34).

2. The hen's care for its chicks

(Matthew 23:37).

3. Vultures (Matthew 24:28).

4. Owl (Psalm 102:6).

5. The parable of the sower (Mark 4:1–20).

6. A pair of doves or two young pigeons (Luke 2:24).

7. Daniel (Daniel 7:4).

8. Eagles (Isaiah 40:31, GNB).

9. The stork (Psalm 104:17).

10. Ravens (1 Kings 17:1–6).

11. A dove (Matthew 3:16).

12. Quail (Exodus 16:13; Numbers 11:31–33).

13. 'Birds that fly by and never settle' (Proverbs 26:2).

14. The ostrich (Job 39:13–16).

15. Sparrows (Matthew 10:31, GNB).

## Plants of the Bible

1. Palm branches (John 12:13).

2. Wild flowers (Matthew 6:28).

3. A sycamore tree (Luke 19:4).

4. Acacia (shittim) wood (Exodus 25:10).

5. Hyssop (John 19:29).

6. Mandrakes; they were popularly thought to have aphrodisiac properties (Genesis 30:14–16).

7. Pomegranates (1 Kings 7:18).

8. Palm; cedars (Psalm 92:12, GNB).

9. Mint, dill, cumin and rue (Matthew 23:23; Luke 11:42).

10. The fig tree (Matthew 21:18–22).

11. Almonds (Numbers 17:1–9).

12. Frankincense and myrrh (Matthew 2:11).

13. An offering of flour, or of unleavened bread, thick loaves or biscuits, or of ears of grain roasted with salt and (except in the case of the sin offering) olive oil (Leviticus 2:1, 4, 13–14; 5:11).

14. Vine (John 15:1–17).

15. Juniper tree (1 Kings 19:4).

16. Myrrh and aloes (John 19:39).

17. The mustard seed (Matthew 13:31; 17:20).

18. Olive; olive; olive (Romans 11:17–18, GNB).

19. Wheat (Exodus 9:32).

20. Flax (Joshua 2:4).

## Dreamers of dreams

1. Joel (Joel 2:28; see also Acts 2:17).

2. The Pharaoh, the wine steward, and the chief baker (Genesis 40–41).

3. Three – all to Joseph; the assurance that he can take Mary as his wife (Matthew 1:20), the command to escape to Egypt (Matthew 2:13), and the command to go to Israel (Matthew 2:19).

4. Solomon, who asked for wisdom (1 Kings 3:5–15).

5. A great stone (Daniel 2:34–35).

6. Nebuchadnezzar himself (Daniel 4:5–33).

7. Jeremiah (23:25, GNB).

8. Pilate's wife (Matthew 27:19).

## ...who shall be nameless

1. His nephew (the son of Paul's sister) (Acts 23:16–24).
2. The Shunammite (a rich woman of Shunem) (2 Kings 4:8–36). Later God used Elisha to save her from death during the famine (2 Kings 8:1–6).
3. Samson's mother; Manoah's wife. The angel later appeared to this woman, and then to her husband. At this second appearance, the husband thought they would die, because they had seen God, but his wife's common sense prevailed (Judges 13).
4. The widow (the widow's mite) (Mark 12:41–44).
5. Lot's wife (Genesis 19:26; Luke 17:32).
6. The woman at the well (John 4:18). She was a Samaritan, a race despised by the Jews, yet her encounter with Jesus led to a number of Samaritan conversions.
7. The Roman army officer on duty at Jesus' crucifixion (Matthew 27:54).

## Colours of the Bible

1. White (as white as light; dazzling white) (Matthew 17:2; Mark 9:3).
2. Purple (Acts 16:14).
3. Red (Matthew 16:2).
4. Green (Mark 6:39).
5. Blue and white (Esther 8:15).
6. Red; red; white (Isaiah 1:18, GNB).
7. Scarlet (Matthew 27:28).
8. Yellow (Leviticus 13:29–37).
9. Grey (Isaiah 46:4).
10. Silver (Genesis 44:2).

## Famous first words

1. John (1:1, GNB).
2. Romans (1:1, GNB).
3. Lamentations (1:1, GNB).
4. Psalm (1:1, GNB).
5. Ruth (1:1, GNB).
6. Acts (1:1, GNB).
7. 3 John (1:1, GNB).
8. Hebrews (1:1, GNB).
9. Genesis (1:1, GNB).
10. Ezekiel (1:1, GNB).
11. Mark (1:1, GNB).
12. Joshua (1:1, GNB).

## The last word

1. Judges (21:25, GNB).
2. 2 Peter (3:18, GNB).
3. Ruth (4:22, GNB).
4. Malachi (4:6, GNB).
5. Daniel (12:13, GNB).
6. John (21:25, GNB).
7. Proverbs (31:31, GNB).
8. Deuteronomy (34:12, GNB).
9. Isaiah (66:24, GNB).
10. 2 Corinthians (13:13, GNB).
11. Nehemiah (13:31, GNB).
12. Jude (25, GNB).

# But God …

1. Joseph, to his brothers (Genesis 50:20, GNB).

2. The LORD speaking to Samuel about the choosing of one of Jesse's sons as king (1 Samuel 16:7, GNB).

3. The suffering of the servant (Isaiah 53:5, GNB).

4. Paul to the Corinthians (1 Corinthians 3:6, GNB).

5. Paul, speaking in the Areopagus in Athens (Acts 17:30, GNB).

6. Paul, in his explanation of the gospel (Romans 3:21, GNB).

7. Paul, in his explanation of the gospel (Romans 6:23, GNB).

8. Paul, describing his work (2 Corinthians 4:12, GNB).

9. Paul, underlining the centrality of the resurrection of Jesus (1 Corinthians 15:20, GNB).

10. Paul, on his 'thorn in the flesh' (2 Corinthians 12:8–9, GNB).

11. Paul, in Galatians 4:4–5 (GNB). (See also Titus 3:4).

12. Paul, describing God's love (Ephesians 2:4–5, GNB).

13. Paul, in Colossians 2:13 (GNB).

14. A description of Christ's sacrifice 'effective for ever' (Hebrews 10:11–12, GNB).

15. Hebrews 1:1–3 (GNB).

# Bible landscapes

1. Ararat range (Genesis 8:4, GNB).

2. Mount Sinai (Deuteronomy 5:1–21, GNB).

3. Mount Hor (Numbers 33:38–39, GNB).

4. Mount Carmel (1 Kings 18:19, GNB).

5. Mount Zion (Hebrews 12:22, GNB)

6. Mount Gilboa (1 Samuel 31:8, GNB).

7. Mount Moriah (2 Chronicles 3:1, GNB).

8. Mount of Olives (Matthew 26:30, GNB).

9. Jordan Valley (Genesis 13:11, GNB).

10. Valley of Salt (2 Samuel 8:13, GNB).

11. Valley of Sorek (Judges 16:4, GNB).

12. Red Sea (Exodus 14:1–22, GNB).

13. Dead Sea (Ezekiel 47:8, GNB).

14. Mediterranean Sea (Joshua 9:1, GNB).

15. Machpelah Cave (Genesis 23:9, GNB).

16. Lake Galilee (Mark 1:16–17, GNB).

17. River Jabbok (Genesis 32:22, GNB).

18. River Nile (Genesis 41:1, GNB).

19. River Jordan (Mark 1:5, GNB).

20. Brook of Cherith (1 Kings 17:5, GNB).

21. Kidron (John 18:1, GNB).

# Put it in writing

1. Revelation (21:27).
2. Ezekiel (2:9–3:3).
3. Ephesus (Acts 19:18–19).
4. The sun standing still and the moon stopping (Joshua 10:13).
5. Paul (2 Timothy 4:13, GNB).

# Chapter and verse

1. Romans 8:28 (GNB).
2. Revelation 3:20 (GNB).
3. Luke 11:11 (GNB).
4. Matthew 7:13–14 (GNB).
5. 2 Peter 1:20 (GNB).
6. Habakkuk 1:13 (GNB).
7. 2 Corinthians 5:17 (GNB).
8. Matthew 1:21 (GNB).
9. Philippians 1:9–11 (GNB).
10. Psalm 24:7 (GNB).
11. Amos 3:3 (GNB).
12. 1 Corinthians 13:12 (GNB).
13. Joel 3:10 (GNB).
14. Mark 8:24 (GNB), the story of Jesus healing a blind man at Bethsaida.
15. Exodus 3:5, (GNB), God speaking to Moses.
16. Micah 6:8 (GNB).
17. Psalm 14:1 (GNB).
18. Proverbs 3:5–6 (GNB).
19. 2 Timothy 2:2 (GNB).
20. Ezekiel 39:14 (GNB).
21. Hebrews 1:14 (GNB).
22. Job 1:21 (GNB).
23. Mark 8:10 (GNB). Dalmanutha is a district on the coast of the Sea of Galilee, perhaps at or adjoining Magadan (or Magdala) (Matthew 15:39).
24. Acts 20:20 (GNB).

# How's your spelling?

1. b) Habakkuk.
2. c) Philippians.
3. a) Zechariah.
4. a) Ecclesiastes.
5. b) Isaiah.

# 3:16's

1. John.
2. 2 Timothy.
3. 1 Corinthians.
4. Malachi.
5. Colossians.

# As it is written …

1. Isaiah 7:14 (GNB).
2. Deuteronomy 8:3 (GNB).
3. Exodus 21:24 (GNB).
4. Zechariah 11:12 (GNB).
5. Leviticus 26:12 (GNB). (See also Genesis 17:7; Exodus 6:7).
6. Zechariah 9:9 (GNB).
7. Psalm 110:1 (GNB).
8. Leviticus 19:18 (GNB).
9. Malachi 3:1 (GNB).
10. Deuteronomy 18:15 (GNB).
11. Isaiah 52:7 (GNB).
12. Hosea 11:1 (GNB).
13. Deuteronomy 21:23 (GNB).
14. Jeremiah 31:31–34 (GNB).
15. Proverbs 25:21–22 (GNB).

# Reading the Bible: the adventure of a lifetime

## Go for it!

A letter arrives from a close friend … you stop what you're doing and eagerly open the envelope. You read the letter through again and again to see what your friend has to say. Perhaps you keep the letter near you, and look at it through the day. You think it over. You feel closer to your friend after reading his or her thoughts.

The Bible's rather like that letter. It's God's letter to us … written by many different human writers, but with one divine author. And just as we get to know our friends more by reading their letters, talking to them and sharing our lives with them, so we get to know God more as we read the Bible and respond to him. We come to know God's thoughts – thoughts that are meant to affect the way we lead our whole lives.

## A daily devotional time

Many Christians over the years have found great benefit in setting aside some time during the day to spend alone with God (some call it a 'quiet time'). Such a time is a daily opportunity to seek the Lord (Psalm 27:8) – a time when God can speak to us 'face to face, just as someone speaks with a friend' (Exodus 33:11).

There are all sorts of problems about having a daily time with God. The main difficulty is making time!

> 'If I were the devil, one of my first aims would be to stop folk from digging into the Bible.'
>
> J.I. Packer, British theologian

Generally speaking, we find time for the things we want to do – think about the things you *do* spend your time on! If a time of Bible reading and prayer is high on our list of personal priorities, then we will make time for it.

When should we read our Bible? In the morning or at night? There can be no hard-and-fast rules. Our circumstances, our jobs and our responsibilities are all different. Some of us are wide awake first thing in the morning, while others are fully conscious only by mid-morning, after several cups of coffee! We each need to work this one out for ourselves and try to read our Bibles and pray at a time of day when we can be sure of being fully alert.

What happens if we miss out on a day or two … or more? You know the answer! You feel guilty … and many Christians feel like that. The devil seems to particularly enjoy taunting Christians with the question, 'How long has it been since you last had a quiet time?' Well, how do we respond to all this? We need to remember that:

(1) 'There is no condemnation now for those who live in union with Christ Jesus' (Romans 8:1, GNB). For us Christians – for those who are in union with Christ – there is *no* condemnation.

(2) We need to seek and know Christ's forgiveness for our lapses into sin.

(3) We may well need to rethink our 'personal timetable', to *make* time for a daily quiet time – to at least *aim* at having one, even if we don't always manage it.

## To be practical …

What 'ingredients' make up a devotional time?

• **Prayer** Stop inwardly and realize that you're coming into the presence of God. Seek his help … seek *him*; worship him. Sometimes we need to repent of hardness of heart or of unforgiveness before we can truly come into God's presence. A psalm or a reading such as Hebrews 10:19–22 may be helpful. Ask the Holy Spirit to speak to you as you read the Bible passage.

• **Reading the Bible** There are many different ways of reading the Bible –

# More precious than gold

The law of the LORD is perfect; it gives new strength. The commands of the LORD are trustworthy, giving wisdom to those who lack it. The laws of the LORD are right, and those who obey them are happy. The commands of the LORD are just and give understanding to the mind.

Reverence for the LORD is good; it will continue for ever. The judgements of the LORD are just; they are always fair. They are more desirable than the finest gold; they are sweeter than the purest honey. They give knowledge to me, your servant; I am rewarded for obeying them.

*Psalm 19:7–11 (GNB)*

for example, reading it chapter by chapter (see pages 154–165), or considering a Bible theme, or looking particularly at the life of one Bible character. And over a period of time variety in one's style of reading may be helpful. But the important thing is that we *do* read the Bible!

There are many different kinds of writing in the Bible (see Bible overview, pages 7–17) and you need to bear this in mind when reading. Whether the passage is poetry, parable or narrative, for example, will affect how we understand it and work out its meaning. (E.g. in a parable, not every tiny detail should be considered to have deep spiritual significance, but instead the main overall meaning should be looked for.) Again the important thing is to read the Bible!

Many people find it helpful to read a booklet or book that will give background details, explanation and other helps. These guides can be

extremely beneficial – as long as we remember to read our Bibles, and not just the accompanying booklet or notes!

It is often useful to ask oneself questions about the passage one is reading. What do I learn about God – Father, Son, and Holy Spirit? What do I learn about people? What are the passage's main characters, actions, themes and purposes? What can I put into practice – are there examples to follow (or avoid)? Are there sins to avoid, warnings to take note of? Are there promises or other truths to lay hold of? Are there further encouragements or challenges to note? Do other passages of the Bible help explain this passage? (A Bible with verse cross-references will be helpful here.) It can be useful to keep a notebook and write down answers and thoughts in it.

Sometimes a verse will spring out of the page and seem to speak directly into our situation. More often we will be encouraged and challenged in a more general way – our lives, lifestyles, attitudes, motives, concerns and prayers being fashioned by God through his word. Sometimes we will want to meditate on – ponder deeply in our hearts as well as in our minds – a particular verse or part of a verse. This is good: in this way God's word becomes part of us. All this, of course, takes time … so it can't really be done effectively in a quick three minutes. (However, even that is much better than nothing, if it is all that we can manage at certain times in our lives, especially if what we read in those three minutes 'impregnates' the rest of the day.)

• **Prayer** Praying after we have read the Scriptures is a natural response to God: he has spoken to us and we in turn speak to him. This is an opportunity both to pray home the message that we have been reading about and also to pray honestly for ourselves and other people. (Of course, this is not the only occasion during the day when we can pray – we can also do it while walking, while waiting in supermarket queues, etc.)

• **Into action!** Our devotional time is 'at the still centre of the turning world'. It's in the world – at college, school or work, in the home, in

'But as for you, continue in the truths that you were taught and firmly believe. You know who your teachers were, and you remember that ever since you were a child, you have known the Holy Scriptures, which are able to give you the wisdom that leads to salvation through faith in Christ Jesus. All Scripture is inspired by God and is useful for teaching the truth, rebuking error, correcting faults, and giving instruction for right living, so that the person who serves God may be fully qualified and equipped to do every kind of good deed.'

Paul, in 2 Timothy 3:14–17 (GNB)

church and in society – that we are to work out, to put into practice, the truths of the Bible that are becoming part of us.

• **Two final do's and don'ts** First, don't hurry through your daily devotional time, but become still! Secondly, don't let it become a mere mechanical duty, but instead seek *God himself* as you read the Bible and pray.

## The adventure of a lifetime

Reading the Bible is like taking part in an adventure ... the adventure of a lifetime ... the adventure of our lives with God. We do not know what our lives have in store for us, but as we turn daily to God's word, we let him speak to us ... encouraging us and also at times challenging us with uncomfortable truths! As we meet with God, we come 'heart to heart' with him. Over the days, over the years, gradually his thoughts become our thoughts, his ways become our ways, and we become 'fully qualified and equipped to do every kind of good deed' (2 Timothy 3:17, GNB).

'Do not deceive yourselves by just listening to his word; instead, put it into practice. Whoever listens to the word but does not put it into practice is like a man who looks in a mirror and sees himself as he is. He takes a good look at himself and then goes away and at once forgets what he looks like. But those who look closely into the perfect law that sets people free, who keep on paying attention to it and do not simply listen and then forget it, but put it into practice – they will be blessed by God in what they do.'

James 1:22–25 (GNB)

# Getting started ... and keeping going

Of all the reasons people mention for not reading the Bible, simple discouragement ranks the highest. People who plan to read the whole Bible, starting with Genesis, often get stuck somewhere around Leviticus, Numbers or Deuteronomy. Others never embark on a reading plan and limit themselves to reading occasionally from familiar passages.

The following three-track plan for reading the Bible is in *The Student Bible: New International Version*. It is designed to break the Bible up into manageable portions. In each of the three tracks, the basic amount to be read is one chapter of the Bible.

• **Track 1** is an introduction to the Bible, consisting of six weeks of readings in the form of three two-week projects.

• **Track 2** gives a survey of every book of the Bible, and covers six months. At least one chapter from every book of the Bible is included.

• **Track 3** covers the whole Bible and is designed to take three years.

If you follow the readings of a particular track, you may find it helpful to put a tick in the box by the side of each chapter number, to remind yourself of where you have reached.

# Track 1: Introduction to the Bible

*Time needed:* Six weeks
*Aim:* To survey basic biblical foundations

Track 1 is a place to begin reading the Bible. Three two-week reading courses take you quickly into passages of the Bible which every Christian should know. These have been selected with two concerns in mind: first, they are frequently quoted or referred to. Second, they are relatively easy to read and understand. Track 1 is a sampler, designed to whet your appetite for more.

## 1. Two weeks on the life and teachings of Jesus

- [ ] Day 1   Luke 1: Preparing for Jesus' arrival
- [ ] Day 2   Luke 2: The story of Jesus' birth
- [ ] Day 3   Mark 1: The beginning of Jesus' ministry
- [ ] Day 4   Mark 9: A day in the life of Jesus
- [ ] Day 5   Matthew 5: The Sermon on the Mount
- [ ] Day 6   Matthew 6: The Sermon on the Mount
- [ ] Day 7   Luke 15: Parables of Jesus
- [ ] Day 8   John 3: A conversation with Jesus
- [ ] Day 9   John 14: Jesus' final instructions
- [ ] Day 10   John 17: Jesus' prayer for his disciples
- [ ] Day 11   Matthew 26: Betrayal and arrest
- [ ] Day 12   Matthew 27: Jesus' execution on a cross
- [ ] Day 13   John 20: Resurrection
- [ ] Day 14   Luke 24: Jesus' appearance after resurrection

## 2. Two weeks on the life and teachings of Paul

- [ ] Day 1   Acts 9: The conversion of Saul
- [ ] Day 2   Acts 16: Paul's Macedonian call and a jailbreak
- [ ] Day 3   Acts 17: Scenes from Paul's missionary journeys
- [ ] Day 4   Acts 26: Paul tells his life-story to a king
- [ ] Day 5   Acts 27: Shipwreck on the way to Rome

☐    Day 6    Acts 28: Paul's arrival in Rome
☐    Day 7    Romans 3: Paul's theology in a nutshell
☐    Day 8    Romans 7: Struggle with sin
☐    Day 9    Romans 8: Life in the Spirit
☐    Day 10   1 Corinthians 13: Paul's description of love
☐    Day 11   1 Corinthians 15: Thoughts on the afterlife
☐    Day 12   Galatians 5: Freedom in Christ
☐    Day 13   Ephesians 3: Paul's summary of his mission
☐    Day 14   Philippians 2: Imitating Christ

## 3. Two weeks on the Old Testament

☐    Day 1    Genesis 1: The story of creation
☐    Day 2    Genesis 3: The origin of sin
☐    Day 3    Genesis 22: Abraham and Isaac
☐    Day 4    Exodus 3: Moses' encounter with God
☐    Day 5    Exodus 20: The gift of the Ten Commandments
☐    Day 6    1 Samuel 17: David and Goliath
☐    Day 7    2 Samuel 11: David and Bathsheba
☐    Day 8    2 Samuel 12: Nathan's rebuke of the king
☐    Day 9    1 Kings 18: Elijah and the prophets of Baal
☐    Day 10   Job 38: God's answer to Job
☐    Day 11   Psalm 51: A classic confession
☐    Day 12   Isaiah 40: Words of comfort from God
☐    Day 13   Daniel 6: Daniel and the lions
☐    Day 14   Amos 4: A prophet's stern warning

# Track 2: Every book in the Bible

*Time needed:* Six months
*Aim:* To gain an overview of the entire Bible

Track 2 includes 189 of the 1,189 chapters in the Bible. Many well-known parts of the Bible are not represented, and from some books (Leviticus, for example), you will read only a single chapter. These 189 chapters have been selected because they are understandable to the average reader without commentary. Taken together, they provide a good foundation of Bible understanding.

If you miss a few days, don't worry. Just resume reading when you can, about a chapter a day. In 181 days you will get an overview that includes something from every book in the Bible.

| | | | | | | |
|---|---|---|---|---|---|---|
| Genesis | ☐ 1 | ☐ 2 | ☐ 3 | ☐ 4 | ☐ 7 | ☐ 8 |
| | ☐ 15 | ☐ 19 | ☐ 22 | ☐ 27 | ☐ 28 | ☐ 37 |
| | ☐ 41 | ☐ 45 | ☐ 50 | | | |
| Exodus | ☐ 3 | ☐ 10–11 | ☐ 14 | ☐ 20 | ☐ 32 | |
| Leviticus | ☐ 26 | | | | | |
| Numbers | ☐ 11 | ☐ 14 | | | | |
| Deuteronomy | ☐ 4 | ☐ 8 | ☐ 28 | | | |
| Joshua | ☐ 2 | ☐ 6 | ☐ 7 | ☐ 24 | | |
| Judges | ☐ 6 | ☐ 7 | ☐ 16 | | | |
| Ruth | ☐ 1 | | | | | |
| 1 Samuel | ☐ 3 | ☐ 16 | ☐ 17 | ☐ 20 | | |
| 2 Samuel | ☐ 6 | ☐ 11 | ☐ 12 | | | |
| 1 Kings | ☐ 3 | ☐ 8 | ☐ 17 | ☐ 18 | | |
| 2 Kings | ☐ 5 | ☐ 17 | ☐ 22 | | | |
| 1 Chronicles | ☐ 17 | | | | | |
| 2 Chronicles | ☐ 20 | ☐ 30 | ☐ 32 | | | |
| Ezra | ☐ 3 | | | | | |
| Nehemiah | ☐ 2 | ☐ 8 | | | | |
| Esther | ☐ 4 | | | | | |

| | | | | | |
|---|---|---|---|---|---|
| Job | ☐ 1–2 | ☐ 38 | ☐ 42 | | |
| Psalms | ☐ 9 | ☐ 23 | ☐ 27 | ☐ 51 | ☐ 84 | ☐ 103 |
| | ☐ 139 | | | | |
| Proverbs | ☐ 4 | ☐ 10 | ☐ 16 | | |
| Ecclesiastes | ☐ 3 | | | | |
| Song of Songs | ☐ 2 | | | | |
| Isaiah | ☐ 6 | ☐ 25 | ☐ 40 | ☐ 52 | ☐ 53 | ☐ 55 |
| Jeremiah | ☐ 2 | ☐ 15 | ☐ 31 | ☐ 38 | | |
| Lamentations | ☐ 3 | | | | |
| Ezekiel | ☐ 1 | ☐ 2–3 | ☐ 4 | ☐ 37 | | |
| Daniel | ☐ 1 | ☐ 3 | ☐ 5 | ☐ 6 | | |
| Hosea | ☐ 2–3 | ☐ 11 | | | | |
| Joel | ☐ 2 | | | | |
| Amos | ☐ 4 | | | | |
| Obadiah | ☐ | | | | |
| Jonah | ☐ 3–4 | | | | |
| Micah | ☐ 6 | | | | |
| Nahum | ☐ 1 | | | | |
| Habakkuk | ☐ 1 | | | | |
| Zephaniah | ☐ 3 | | | | |
| Haggai | ☐ 1 | | | | |
| Zechariah | ☐ 8 | | | | |
| Malachi | ☐ 3 | | | | |
| Matthew | ☐ 5 | ☐ 6 | ☐ 13 | ☐ 19 | ☐ 26 | ☐ 27 |
| | ☐ 28 | | | | |
| Mark | ☐ 1 | ☐ 2 | ☐ 3 | ☐ 4 | ☐ 5 | ☐ 6 |
| | ☐ 7 | ☐ 8 | ☐ 9 | ☐ 10 | ☐ 11 | ☐ 12 |
| | ☐ 13 | ☐ 14 | ☐ 15–16 | | | |
| Luke | ☐ 1 | ☐ 2 | ☐ 10 | ☐ 12 | ☐ 15 | ☐ 16 |
| | ☐ 18 | ☐ 24 | | | | |
| John | ☐ 3 | ☐ 6 | ☐ 10 | ☐ 14 | ☐ 15 | ☐ 16 |
| | ☐ 17 | ☐ 20 | | | | |
| Acts | ☐ 1 | ☐ 2 | ☐ 5 | ☐ 9 | ☐ 16 | ☐ 17 |
| | ☐ 26 | ☐ 27 | ☐ 28 | | | |
| Romans | ☐ 3 | ☐ 7 | ☐ 8 | ☐ 12 | | |
| 1 Corinthians | ☐ 13 | ☐ 15 | | | | |
| 2 Corinthians | ☐ 4 | ☐ 12 | | | | |

| Galatians | ☐ 3 | | |
| Ephesians | ☐ 2 | ☐ 3 | |
| Philippians | ☐ 2 | | |
| Colossians | ☐ 1 | | |
| 1 Thessalonians | ☐ 3–4 | | |
| 2 Thessalonians | ☐ 2 | | |
| 1 Timothy | ☐ 1 | | |
| 2 Timothy | ☐ 2 | | |
| Titus | ☐ 2 | | |
| Philemon | ☐ | | |
| Hebrews | ☐ 2 | ☐ 11 | ☐ 12 |
| James | ☐ 1 | | |
| 1 Peter | ☐ 1 | | |
| 2 Peter | ☐ 1 | | |
| 1 John | ☐ 3 | | |
| 2 and 3 John | ☐ | | |
| Jude | ☐ | | |
| Revelation | ☐ 1 | ☐ 12 | ☐ 21 |

# Track 3: The whole Bible

*Time needed:* Three years
*Aim:* To read all the way through the Bible

Track 3 takes you completely through the Bible, reading every word. Other Bible-reading plans allot only a year for this project, requiring that at least three chapters be read each day. But many readers find such a pace to be unrealistic and discouraging. For this reason, Track 3 assigns usually only one chapter a day. (Some short chapters have been combined, so occasionally you will read two brief chapters in a day.) In all, the reading plan works out evenly to a three-year total. The Track 3 plan alternates between the Old Testament and New Testament. This mixing provides variety and reduces the fatigue that may set in from reading long sections of the Old Testament.

| Genesis | | | | |
|---|---|---|---|---|
| | ☐ 1 | ☐ 2 | ☐ 3 | ☐ 4 |
| | ☐ 5 | ☐ 6 | ☐ 7 | ☐ 8 |
| | ☐ 9 | ☐ 10–11 | ☐ 12 | ☐ 13 |
| | ☐ 14 | ☐ 15 | ☐ 16 | ☐ 17 |
| | ☐ 18 | ☐ 19 | ☐ 20 | ☐ 21 |
| | ☐ 22 | ☐ 23 | ☐ 24 | ☐ 25 |
| | ☐ 26 | ☐ 27 | ☐ 28 | ☐ 29 |
| | ☐ 30 | ☐ 31 | ☐ 32 | ☐ 33 |
| | ☐ 34 | ☐ 35 | ☐ 36 | ☐ 37 |
| | ☐ 38 | ☐ 39 | ☐ 40 | ☐ 41 |
| | ☐ 42 | ☐ 43 | ☐ 44 | ☐ 45 |
| | ☐ 46 | ☐ 47 | ☐ 48 | ☐ 49 |
| | ☐ 50 | | | |
| Matthew 1–9 | ☐ 1 | ☐ 2 | ☐ 3 | ☐ 4 |
| | ☐ 5 | ☐ 6 | ☐ 7 | ☐ 8 |
| | ☐ 9 | | | |
| Exodus | ☐ 1 | ☐ 2 | ☐ 3 | ☐ 4 |
| | ☐ 5 | ☐ 6 | ☐ 7 | ☐ 8 |

|  | | | |
|---|---|---|---|
| | ☐ 9 | ☐ 10–11 | ☐ 12 | ☐ 13 |
| | ☐ 14 | ☐ 15 | ☐ 16 | ☐ 17 |
| | ☐ 18 | ☐ 19 | ☐ 20 | ☐ 21 |
| | ☐ 22 | ☐ 23 | ☐ 24 | ☐ 25 |
| | ☐ 26 | ☐ 27 | ☐ 28 | ☐ 29 |
| | ☐ 30 | ☐ 31 | ☐ 32 | ☐ 33 |
| | ☐ 34 | ☐ 35 | ☐ 36 | ☐ 37 |
| | ☐ 38 | ☐ 39 | ☐ 40 | |
| **Matthew 10–20** | ☐ 10 | ☐ 11 | ☐ 12 | ☐ 13 |
| | ☐ 14 | ☐ 15 | ☐ 16 | ☐ 17 |
| | ☐ 18 | ☐ 19 | ☐ 20 | |
| **Leviticus 1–14** | ☐ 1 | ☐ 2 | ☐ 3 | ☐ 4 |
| | ☐ 5 | ☐ 6 | ☐ 7 | ☐ 8 |
| | ☐ 9 | ☐ 10 | ☐ 11–12 | ☐ 13 |
| | ☐ 14 | | | |
| **Matthew 21–28** | ☐ 21 | ☐ 22 | ☐ 23 | ☐ 24 |
| | ☐ 25 | ☐ 26 | ☐ 27 | ☐ 28 |
| **Leviticus 15–27** | ☐ 15 | ☐ 16 | ☐ 17 | ☐ 18 |
| | ☐ 19 | ☐ 20 | ☐ 21 | ☐ 22 |
| | ☐ 23 | ☐ 24 | ☐ 25 | ☐ 26 |
| | ☐ 27 | | | |
| **Mark 1–8** | ☐ 1 | ☐ 2 | ☐ 3 | ☐ 4 |
| | ☐ 5 | ☐ 6 | ☐ 7 | ☐ 8 |
| **Numbers** | ☐ 1–2 | ☐ 3 | ☐ 4 | ☐ 5 |
| | ☐ 6 | ☐ 7 | ☐ 8 | ☐ 9 |
| | ☐ 10 | ☐ 11 | ☐ 12 | ☐ 13 |
| | ☐ 14 | ☐ 15 | ☐ 16 | ☐ 17 |
| | ☐ 18 | ☐ 19 | ☐ 20 | ☐ 21 |
| | ☐ 22 | ☐ 23 | ☐ 24 | ☐ 25 |
| | ☐ 26 | ☐ 27 | ☐ 28 | ☐ 29 |
| | ☐ 30 | ☐ 31 | ☐ 32 | ☐ 33 |
| | ☐ 34 | ☐ 35 | ☐ 36 | |
| **Mark 9–16** | ☐ 9 | ☐ 10 | ☐ 11 | ☐ 12 |
| | ☐ 13 | ☐ 14 | ☐ 15–16 | |
| **Deuteronomy 1–17** | ☐ 1 | ☐ 2 | ☐ 3 | ☐ 4 |
| | ☐ 5 | ☐ 6 | ☐ 7 | ☐ 8 |
| | ☐ 9 | ☐ 10 | ☐ 11 | ☐ 12 |

|  | | | |
|---|---|---|---|
| | ☐ 13 | ☐ 14 | ☐ 15 | ☐ 16 |
| | ☐ 17 | | | |
| Luke 1–8 | ☐ 1 | ☐ 2 | ☐ 3 | ☐ 4 |
| | ☐ 5 | ☐ 6 | ☐ 7 | ☐ 8 |
| Deuteronomy 18–34 | ☐ 18 | ☐ 19 | ☐ 20 | ☐ 21 |
| | ☐ 22 | ☐ 23 | ☐ 24 | ☐ 25 |
| | ☐ 26 | ☐ 27 | ☐ 28 | ☐ 29 |
| | ☐ 30 | ☐ 31 | ☐ 32 | ☐ 33 |
| | ☐ 34 | | | |
| Luke 9–16 | ☐ 9 | ☐ 10 | ☐ 11 | ☐ 12 |
| | ☐ 13 | ☐ 14 | ☐ 15 | ☐ 16 |
| Joshua | ☐ 1 | ☐ 2 | ☐ 3 | ☐ 4 |
| | ☐ 5 | ☐ 6 | ☐ 7 | ☐ 8 |
| | ☐ 9 | ☐ 10 | ☐ 11 | ☐ 12–13 |
| | ☐ 14–15 | ☐ 16–17 | ☐ 18 | ☐ 19 |
| | ☐ 20 | ☐ 21 | ☐ 22 | ☐ 23 |
| | ☐ 24 | | | |
| Luke 17–24 | ☐ 17 | ☐ 18 | ☐ 19 | ☐ 20 |
| | ☐ 21 | ☐ 22 | ☐ 23 | ☐ 24 |
| Judges | ☐ 1 | ☐ 2 | ☐ 3 | ☐ 4 |
| | ☐ 5 | ☐ 6 | ☐ 7 | ☐ 8 |
| | ☐ 9 | ☐ 10 | ☐ 11 | ☐ 12 |
| | ☐ 13 | ☐ 14 | ☐ 15 | ☐ 16 |
| | ☐ 17 | ☐ 18 | ☐ 19 | ☐ 20 |
| | ☐ 21 | | | |
| John 1–7 | ☐ 1 | ☐ 2 | ☐ 3 | ☐ 4 |
| | ☐ 5 | ☐ 6 | ☐ 7 | |
| Ruth | ☐ 1 | ☐ 2 | ☐ 3 | ☐ 4 |
| 1 Samuel 1–15 | ☐ 1 | ☐ 2 | ☐ 3 | ☐ 4 |
| | ☐ 5 | ☐ 6 | ☐ 7 | ☐ 8 |
| | ☐ 9 | ☐ 10 | ☐ 11 | ☐ 12 |
| | ☐ 13 | ☐ 14 | ☐ 15 | |
| John 8–14 | ☐ 8 | ☐ 9 | ☐ 10 | ☐ 11 |
| | ☐ 12 | ☐ 13 | ☐ 14 | |
| 1 Samuel 16–31 | ☐ 16 | ☐ 17 | ☐ 18 | ☐ 19 |
| | ☐ 20 | ☐ 21 | ☐ 22 | ☐ 23 |
| | ☐ 24 | ☐ 25 | ☐ 26 | ☐ 27 |

| | | | | |
|---|---|---|---|---|
| | ☐ 28 | ☐ 29 | ☐ 30 | ☐ 31 |
| John 15–21 | ☐ 15 | ☐ 16 | ☐ 17 | ☐ 18 |
| | ☐ 19 | ☐ 20 | ☐ 21 | |
| 2 Samuel | ☐ 1 | ☐ 2 | ☐ 3 | ☐ 4 |
| | ☐ 5 | ☐ 6 | ☐ 7 | ☐ 8 |
| | ☐ 9 | ☐ 10 | ☐ 11 | ☐ 12 |
| | ☐ 13 | ☐ 14 | ☐ 15 | ☐ 16 |
| | ☐ 17 | ☐ 18 | ☐ 19 | ☐ 20 |
| | ☐ 21 | ☐ 22 | ☐ 23 | ☐ 24 |
| Acts 1–7 | ☐ 1 | ☐ 2 | ☐ 3 | ☐ 4 |
| | ☐ 5 | ☐ 6 | ☐ 7 | |
| 1 Kings 1–11 | ☐ 1 | ☐ 2 | ☐ 3 | ☐ 4–5 |
| | ☐ 6 | ☐ 7 | ☐ 8 | ☐ 9 |
| | ☐ 10 | ☐ 11 | | |
| Acts 8–14 | ☐ 8 | ☐ 9 | ☐ 10 | ☐ 11 |
| | ☐ 12 | ☐ 13 | ☐ 14 | |
| 1 Kings 12–22 | ☐ 12 | ☐ 13 | ☐ 14 | ☐ 15 |
| | ☐ 16 | ☐ 17 | ☐ 18 | ☐ 19 |
| | ☐ 20 | ☐ 21 | ☐ 22 | |
| Acts 15–21 | ☐ 15 | ☐ 16 | ☐ 17 | ☐ 18 |
| | ☐ 19 | ☐ 20 | ☐ 21 | |
| 2 Kings | ☐ 1 | ☐ 2 | ☐ 3 | ☐ 4 |
| | ☐ 5 | ☐ 6 | ☐ 7 | ☐ 8 |
| | ☐ 9 | ☐ 10 | ☐ 11 | ☐ 12 |
| | ☐ 13 | ☐ 14 | ☐ 15 | ☐ 16 |
| | ☐ 17 | ☐ 18 | ☐ 19 | ☐ 20 |
| | ☐ 21 | ☐ 22 | ☐ 23 | ☐ 24 |
| | ☐ 25 | | | |
| Acts 22–28 | ☐ 22 | ☐ 23 | ☐ 24 | ☐ 25 |
| | ☐ 26 | ☐ 27 | ☐ 28 | |
| 1 Chronicles 1–14 | ☐ 1–9 | ☐ 10 | ☐ 11 | ☐ 12 |
| | ☐ 13 | ☐ 14 | | |
| Romans 1–8 | ☐ 1 | ☐ 2 | ☐ 3 | ☐ 4 |
| | ☐ 5 | ☐ 6 | ☐ 7 | ☐ 8 |
| 1 Chronicles 15–29 | ☐ 15 | ☐ 16 | ☐ 17 | ☐ 18 |
| | ☐ 19 | ☐ 20 | ☐ 21 | ☐ 22 |
| | ☐ 23–27 | ☐ 28 | ☐ 29 | |

| Romans 9–16 | ☐ 9 | ☐ 10 | ☐ 11 | ☐ 12–13 |
|---|---|---|---|---|
| | ☐ 14 | ☐ 15–16 | | |
| 2 Chronicles 1–18 | ☐ 1 | ☐ 2 | ☐ 3 | ☐ 4 |
| | ☐ 5 | ☐ 6 | ☐ 7 | ☐ 8 |
| | ☐ 9 | ☐ 10 | ☐ 11 | ☐ 12 |
| | ☐ 13 | ☐ 14 | ☐ 15 | ☐ 16–17 |
| | ☐ 18 | | | |
| 1 Corinthians 1–9 | ☐ 1 | ☐ 2 | ☐ 3 | ☐ 4–5 |
| | ☐ 6 | ☐ 7 | ☐ 8–9 | |
| 2 Chronicles 19–36 | ☐ 19 | ☐ 20 | ☐ 21 | ☐ 22 |
| | ☐ 23 | ☐ 24 | ☐ 25 | ☐ 26–7 |
| | ☐ 28 | ☐ 29 | ☐ 30 | ☐ 31 |
| | ☐ 32 | ☐ 33 | ☐ 34 | ☐ 35 |
| | ☐ 36 | | | |
| 1 Corinthians 10–16 | ☐ 10 | ☐ 11 | ☐ 12 | ☐ 13 |
| | ☐ 14 | ☐ 15 | ☐ 16 | |
| Ezra | ☐ 1–2 | ☐ 3 | ☐ 4 | ☐ 5 |
| | ☐ 6 | ☐ 7 | ☐ 8 | ☐ 9 |
| | ☐ 10 | | | |
| Nehemiah | ☐ 1 | ☐ 2–3 | ☐ 4 | ☐ 5 |
| | ☐ 6 | ☐ 7 | ☐ 8 | ☐ 9 |
| | ☐ 10 | ☐ 11 | ☐ 12 | ☐ 13 |
| 2 Corinthians | ☐ 1 | ☐ 2–3 | ☐ 4 | ☐ 5 |
| | ☐ 6 | ☐ 7 | ☐ 8–9 | ☐ 10 |
| | ☐ 11 | ☐ 12–13 | | |
| Esther | ☐ 1 | ☐ 2 | ☐ 3 | ☐ 4 |
| | ☐ 5 | ☐ 6–7 | ☐ 8 | ☐ 9–10 |
| Job 1–21 | ☐ 1 | ☐ 2 | ☐ 3 | ☐ 4 |
| | ☐ 5 | ☐ 6 | ☐ 7 | ☐ 8 |
| | ☐ 9 | ☐ 10 | ☐ 11 | ☐ 12 |
| | ☐ 13 | ☐ 14 | ☐ 15 | ☐ 16 |
| | ☐ 17 | ☐ 18 | ☐ 19 | ☐ 20 |
| | ☐ 21 | | | |
| Galatians | ☐ 1 | ☐ 2 | ☐ 3 | ☐ 4 |
| | ☐ 5–6 | | | |
| Job 22–42 | ☐ 22 | ☐ 23 | ☐ 24 | ☐ 25–26 |
| | ☐ 27 | ☐ 28 | ☐ 29 | ☐ 30 |

|  | □ 31 | □ 32 | □ 33 | □ 34 |
|---|---|---|---|---|
|  | □ 35 | □ 36 | □ 37 | □ 38 |
|  | □ 39 | □ 40 | □ 41 | □ 42 |
| Ephesians | □ 1 | □ 2 | □ 3 | □ 4 |
|  | □ 5 | □ 6 |  |  |
| Psalms 1–40 | □ 1–2 | □ 3–4 | □ 5 | □ 6 |
|  | □ 7 | □ 8 | □ 9 | □ 10 |
|  | □ 11–12 | □ 13–14 | □ 15–16 | □ 17 |
|  | □ 18 | □ 19 | □ 20–21 | □ 22 |
|  | □ 23–24 | □ 25 | □ 26 | □ 27 |
|  | □ 28–29 | □ 30 | □ 31 | □ 32 |
|  | □ 33 | □ 34 | □ 35 | □ 36 |
|  | □ 37 | □ 38 | □ 39 | □ 40 |
| Philippians | □ 1 | □ 2 | □ 3 | □ 4 |
| Psalms 41–80 | □ 41 | □ 42–43 | □ 44 | □ 45 |
|  | □ 46–47 | □ 48 | □ 49 | □ 50 |
|  | □ 51 | □ 52 | □ 53–54 | □ 55 |
|  | □ 56 | □ 57 | □ 58 | □ 59 |
|  | □ 60–61 | □ 62 | □ 63–64 | □ 65 |
|  | □ 66 | □ 67 | □ 68 | □ 69 |
|  | □ 70 | □ 71 | □ 72 | □ 73 |
|  | □ 74 | □ 75 | □ 76 | □ 77 |
|  | □ 78 | □ 79 | □ 80 |  |
| Colossians | □ 1 | □ 2 | □ 3 | □ 4 |
| Psalms 81–118 | □ 81 | □ 82 | □ 83 | □ 84 |
|  | □ 85 | □ 86 | □ 87 | □ 88 |
|  | □ 89 | □ 90 | □ 91 | □ 92–93 |
|  | □ 94 | □ 95 | □ 96 | □ 97 |
|  | □ 98–99 | □ 100–101 | □ 102 | □ 103 |
|  | □ 104 | □ 105 | □ 106 | □ 107 |
|  | □ 108 | □ 109 | □ 110–111 | □ 112–113 |
|  | □ 114 | □ 115 | □ 116–117 | □ 118 |
| Psalm 119 | □ 1–48 | □ 49–96 | □ 97–144 | □ 145–176 |
| Psalms 120–121 | □ |  |  |  |
| 1 Thessalonians | □ 1–2 | □ 3–4 | □ 5 |  |
| 2 Thessalonians | □ 1–2 | □ 3 |  |  |
| Psalms 122–150 | □ 122–123 | □ 124–125 | □ 126–128 | □ 129–130 |

|  | | | |
|---|---|---|---|
|  | ☐ 131–132 | ☐ 133–134 | ☐ 135 | ☐ 136 |
|  | ☐ 137–138 | ☐ 139 | ☐ 140 | ☐ 141–142 |
|  | ☐ 143 | ☐ 144 | ☐ 145 | ☐ 146 |
|  | ☐ 147 | ☐ 148 | ☐ 149–150 | |
| Proverbs | ☐ 1 | ☐ 2 | ☐ 3 | ☐ 4 |
|  | ☐ 5 | ☐ 6 | ☐ 7 | ☐ 8 |
|  | ☐ 9 | ☐ 10 | ☐ 11 | ☐ 12 |
|  | ☐ 13 | ☐ 14 | ☐ 15 | ☐ 16 |
|  | ☐ 17 | ☐ 18 | ☐ 19 | ☐ 20 |
|  | ☐ 21 | ☐ 22 | ☐ 23 | ☐ 24 |
|  | ☐ 25 | ☐ 26 | ☐ 27 | ☐ 28 |
|  | ☐ 29 | ☐ 30 | ☐ 31 | |
| 1 Timothy | ☐ 1–2 | ☐ 3–4 | ☐ 5 | ☐ 6 |
| Ecclesiastes | ☐ 1 | ☐ 2 | ☐ 3 | ☐ 4 |
|  | ☐ 5 | ☐ 6 | ☐ 7 | ☐ 8 |
|  | ☐ 9 | ☐ 10 | ☐ 11 | ☐ 12 |
| Song of Songs | ☐ 1 | ☐ 2 | ☐ 3 | ☐ 4 |
|  | ☐ 5 | ☐ 6 | ☐ 7 | ☐ 8 |
| 2 Timothy | ☐ 1 | ☐ 2 | ☐ 3 | ☐ 4 |
| Isaiah 1–36 | ☐ 1 | ☐ 2 | ☐ 3 | ☐ 4–5 |
|  | ☐ 6 | ☐ 7 | ☐ 8 | ☐ 9 |
|  | ☐ 10 | ☐ 11 | ☐ 12 | ☐ 13 |
|  | ☐ 14 | ☐ 15 | ☐ 16 | ☐ 17 |
|  | ☐ 18 | ☐ 19–20 | ☐ 21 | ☐ 22 |
|  | ☐ 23 | ☐ 24 | ☐ 25 | ☐ 26 |
|  | ☐ 27 | ☐ 28 | ☐ 29 | ☐ 30 |
|  | ☐ 31 | ☐ 32 | ☐ 33 | ☐ 34 |
|  | ☐ 35 | ☐ 36 | | |
| Titus | ☐ 1 | ☐ 2–3 | | |
| Isaiah 37–66 | ☐ 37 | ☐ 38–39 | ☐ 40 | ☐ 41 |
|  | ☐ 42 | ☐ 43 | ☐ 44 | ☐ 45 |
|  | ☐ 46 | ☐ 47 | ☐ 48 | ☐ 49 |
|  | ☐ 50 | ☐ 51 | ☐ 52 | ☐ 53 |
|  | ☐ 54 | ☐ 55 | ☐ 56 | ☐ 57 |
|  | ☐ 58 | ☐ 59 | ☐ 60 | ☐ 61 |
|  | ☐ 62 | ☐ 63 | ☐ 64 | ☐ 65 |
|  | ☐ 66 | | | |

| | | | | |
|---|---|---|---|---|
| Philemon | ☐ | | | |
| Jeremiah 1–26 | ☐ 1 | ☐ 2 | ☐ 3 | ☐ 4 |
| | ☐ 5 | ☐ 6 | ☐ 7 | ☐ 8 |
| | ☐ 9 | ☐ 10 | ☐ 11 | ☐ 12 |
| | ☐ 13 | ☐ 14 | ☐ 15 | ☐ 16 |
| | ☐ 17 | ☐ 18 | ☐ 19 | ☐ 20 |
| | ☐ 21 | ☐ 22 | ☐ 23 | ☐ 24 |
| | ☐ 25 | ☐ 26 | | |
| Hebrews 1–7 | ☐ 1 | ☐ 2 | ☐ 3–4 | ☐ 5–6 |
| | ☐ 7 | | | |
| Jeremiah 27–52 | ☐ 27 | ☐ 28 | ☐ 29 | ☐ 30 |
| | ☐ 31 | ☐ 32 | ☐ 33 | ☐ 34 |
| | ☐ 35 | ☐ 36 | ☐ 37 | ☐ 38 |
| | ☐ 39 | ☐ 40 | ☐ 41 | ☐ 42 |
| | ☐ 43 | ☐ 44 | ☐ 44–45 | ☐ 46 |
| | ☐ 47 | ☐ 48 | ☐ 49 | ☐ 50 |
| | ☐ 51 | ☐ 52 | | |
| Hebrews 8–13 | ☐ 8 | ☐ 9 | ☐ 10 | ☐ 11 |
| | ☐ 12 | ☐ 13 | | |
| Lamentations | ☐ 1 | ☐ 2 | ☐ 3 | ☐ 4 |
| | ☐ 5 | | | |
| Ezekiel 1–24 | ☐ 1 | ☐ 2–3 | ☐ 4 | ☐ 5 |
| | ☐ 6 | ☐ 7 | ☐ 8 | ☐ 9 |
| | ☐ 10 | ☐ 11 | ☐ 12 | ☐ 13 |
| | ☐ 14 | ☐ 15 | ☐ 16 | ☐ 17 |
| | ☐ 18 | ☐ 19 | ☐ 20 | ☐ 21 |
| | ☐ 22 | ☐ 23 | ☐ 24 | |
| James | ☐ 1 | ☐ 2 | ☐ 3–4 | ☐ 5 |
| Ezekiel 25–48 | ☐ 25 | ☐ 26 | ☐ 27 | ☐ 28 |
| | ☐ 29 | ☐ 30 | ☐ 31 | ☐ 32 |
| | ☐ 33 | ☐ 34 | ☐ 35 | ☐ 36 |
| | ☐ 37 | ☐ 38 | ☐ 39 | ☐ 40 |
| | ☐ 41 | ☐ 42 | ☐ 43 | ☐ 44 |
| | ☐ 45 | ☐ 46 | ☐ 47 | ☐ 48 |
| 1 Peter | ☐ 1 | ☐ 2 | ☐ 3 | ☐ 4–5 |
| Daniel | ☐ 1 | ☐ 2 | ☐ 3 | ☐ 4 |
| | ☐ 5 | ☐ 6 | ☐ 7 | ☐ 8 |

|  | | | |
|---|---|---|---|
|  | ☐ 9 | ☐ 10 | ☐ 11 | ☐ 12 |
| 2 Peter | ☐ 1 | ☐ 2 | ☐ 3 | |
| Hosea | ☐ 1 | ☐ 2–3 | ☐ 4 | ☐ 5 |
|  | ☐ 6–7 | ☐ 8 | ☐ 9 | ☐ 10 |
|  | ☐ 11–12 | ☐ 13–14 | | |
| 1 John | ☐ 1–2 | ☐ 3 | ☐ 4 | ☐ 5 |
| Joel | ☐ 1 | ☐ 2 | ☐ 3 | |
| Amos | ☐ 1 | ☐ 2 | ☐ 3 | ☐ 4 |
|  | ☐ 5 | ☐ 6 | ☐ 7 | ☐ 8 |
|  | ☐ 9 | | | |
| Obadiah | ☐ | | | |
| Jonah | ☐ 1–2 | ☐ 3–4 | | |
| 2 and 3 John | ☐ | | | |
| Micah | ☐ 1 | ☐ 2 | ☐ 3 | ☐ 4 |
|  | ☐ 5 | ☐ 6 | ☐ 7 | |
| Nahum | ☐ 1 | ☐ 2 | ☐ 3 | |
| Jude | ☐ | | | |
| Habakkuk | ☐ 1 | ☐ 2 | ☐ 3 | |
| Zephaniah | ☐ 1 | ☐ 2 | ☐ 3 | |
| Revelation 1–7 | ☐ 1 | ☐ 2 | ☐ 3 | ☐ 4–5 |
|  | ☐ 6 | ☐ 7 | | |
| Haggai | ☐ 1 | ☐ 2 | | |
| Revelation 8–14 | ☐ 8 | ☐ 9 | ☐ 10–11 | ☐ 12 |
|  | ☐ 13 | ☐ 14 | | |
| Zechariah | ☐ 1 | ☐ 2–3 | ☐ 4–5 | ☐ 6 |
|  | ☐ 7 | ☐ 8 | ☐ 9 | ☐ 10 |
|  | ☐ 11 | ☐ 12–13 | ☐ 14 | |
| Malachi | ☐ 1 | ☐ 2 | ☐ 3–4 | |
| Revelation 15–22 | ☐ 15–16 | ☐ 17 | ☐ 18 | ☐ 19 |
|  | ☐ 20 | ☐ 21 | ☐ 22 | |

# Where to find ...

## Well-known events

Creation, Genesis 1–2
The first sin, or fall, Genesis 3
Cain kills Abel, Genesis 4
Noah and the ark, Genesis 6–9
Sodom and Gomorrah, Genesis
   18–19
Abraham sacrifices Isaac, Genesis 22
Jacob's ladder, Genesis 28:10–22
Joseph and the coat, Genesis 37
Moses' birth, Exodus 2
Moses and the burning bush,
   Exodus 3
Plagues on Egypt, Exodus 7–11
The Exodus, Exodus 12–13
The Ten Commandments, Exodus 20
The battle of Jericho, Joshua 6
Gideon and the fleece, Judges 6–7
Samson and Delilah, Judges 13–16
God calls the boy Samuel, 1 Samuel
   1–3
David and Goliath, 1 Samuel 17
David and Bathsheba, 2 Samuel 11
Elijah versus the priests of Baal,
   1 Kings 18
Elisha's miracles, 2 Kings 4–5
Ezekiel and the dry bones, Ezekiel 37
Daniel in the lions' den, Daniel 6
Hosea and his adulterous wife, Hosea
   1–3
Jonah and the fish, Jonah 1

Birth of Jesus, Luke 1–2
Baptism of Jesus, Mark 1:9–11
Temptation of Jesus, Luke 4:1–13
Jesus clears the temple, John 2:12–25
The transfiguration of Jesus, Matthew
   17:1–13
Jesus raises Lazarus from the dead,
   John 11:1–46
Jesus' triumphal entry into Jerusalem,
   Mark 11:1–11
Jesus and the widow's offering, Mark
   12:41–44
The Last Supper, Luke 22:7–38
Jesus washes his disciples' feet, John
   13:1–17
Jesus at Gethsemane, Matthew
   26:36–56
Judas betrays Jesus, Luke 22:1–53
Peter denies Christ, Luke 22:54–62
The crucifixion, Matthew
   26:57–27:66
The resurrection and ascension,
   Luke 24
The Holy Spirit at Pentecost, Acts 2
Stephen stoned, Acts 6–7
Paul's conversion, Acts 9:1–31
Peter's escape from prison, Acts
   12:1–19
Paul and Silas in prison, Acts
   16:16–40

# Jesus' teachings

Beatitudes, Matthew 5:1–12

Bread of life, John 6:25–59

Born again, John 3:1–21

Discipleship, Luke 14:25–35

Give to Caesar, Mark 12:13–17

Good Shepherd, John 10:1–21

Golden rule, Luke 6:31

Greatest commandment, Matthew 22:34–40

Living water, John 4:1–26

Lord's prayer, Matthew 6:5–15

Sending out the Twelve, Matthew 10

Sermon on the Mount, Matthew 5–7

Vine and branches, John 15:1–17

The way, the truth, and the life, John 14:5–14

Wealth, Matthew 19:16–30

Worry, Luke 12:22–34

# Prayers of the Bible

Abraham's prayer for Sodom, Genesis 18:22–33

Isaac's blessing, Genesis 27

Jacob's desperate prayer at Penuel, Genesis 32

Jacob blesses his sons, Genesis 48–49

Moses' song of thanksgiving for deliverance from Egypt, Exodus 15

Moses' plea for Israel when they had worshipped the golden calf, Exodus 32; Deuteronomy 9

Moses asks to see God's glory, Exodus 33

Aaron's blessing, Numbers 6

Moses' song: God and his people, Deuteronomy 32

Moses blesses the people of Israel, Deuteronomy 33

Deborah's song of thanksgiving for victory, Judges 5

Gideon's prayer for signs, Judges 6

Hannah's prayer for a son, 1 Samuel 1; her thanksgiving, 1 Samuel 2

Samuel's prayer for the nation, 1 Samuel 7

David's prayer following God's promise of a lasting succession, 2 Samuel 7; 1 Chronicles 17

David's song of thanksgiving for deliverance, 2 Samuel 22; Psalm 18

Solomon's prayer for wisdom, 1 Kings 3; 2 Chronicles 1

Solomon's prayer at the dedication of the temple, 1 Kings 8, 2 Chronicles 6

Elijah's prayer on Mount Carmel, 1 Kings 18

Elijah and the 'still small voice' ('soft whisper'), 1 Kings 19

Hezekiah's prayer at the time of Sennacherib's siege, 2 Kings 19; Isaiah 37

Thanksgiving as the Covenant Box is brought to Jerusalem, 1 Chronicles 16

David's prayer for Solomon, 1 Chronicles 29

Ezra's confession of the nation's sin, Ezra 9

Nehemiah's prayer for his people,
   Nehemiah 1
The public confession led by Ezra,
   Nehemiah 9
Job seeks the reason for his suffering,
   Job 10
Job pleads his case, Job 13–14
Job's confession, Job 42

## The Psalms include an enormous number of prayers: some are listed here, under themes:

Evening and morning prayer, 4, 5
The shepherd psalm, 23
Praise and worship, 24; 67; 92;
   95–98; 100; 113; 145; 148; 150
Guidance and trust, 25; 37; 62
Deliverance, 40; 116
Longing for God, 27; 42; 63; 84
Forgiveness, 51; 130
Thanksgiving, 65; 111; 136
Help in trouble, 69; 86; 88; 102; 140;
   143
God's constant love and care, 89; 103;
   107; 146
God's majesty and glory, 8; 29; 93
God's knowledge and presence, 139
God's word, 19; 119
God's protection, 46; 91; 125

Prayers of Isaiah, Isaiah 25; 33; 63–64
Hezekiah's prayer in his illness,
   Isaiah 38
Jeremiah's prayers, Jeremiah 11; 14;
   20; 32

The King's dream: Daniel's prayer,
   Daniel 2
Nebuchadnezzar praises God,
   Daniel 4
Daniel's prayer at the end of the exile,
   Daniel 9
Jonah's prayer, Jonah 2
Habakkuk questions God and prays
   to him, Habakkuk 1 and 3

## Prayers of Jesus:

The Lord's Prayer, Matthew 6:9–13;
   Luke 11:2–4
In the Garden of Gethsemane,
   Matthew 26:36–44; Mark
   14:32–39; Luke 22:46
From the cross, Matthew 27:46; Mark
   15:34; Luke 23:34, 46
At the raising of Lazarus, John
   11:41–42
Facing death, John 12:27–28
For his followers, John 17

Mary's thanksgiving (Magnificat),
   Luke 1:46–55
Zechariah's prayer (Benedictus),
   Luke 1:68–79
Simeon's prayer (Nunc Dimittis),
   Luke 2:29–35
Prayers of the Pharisee and the tax
   collector, Luke 18:10–13
The church's prayer in the face of
   threats, Acts 4:24–30
Stephen's prayer at his death, Acts
   7:59–60

## Prayers of Paul:

For the Christians at Rome, Romans 1:8–10

For Israel, Romans 10:1

For the church at Corinth,
1 Corinthians 1:4–9
2 Corinthians 13:7–9

Thanksgiving for God's comfort in trouble, 2 Corinthians 1:3–4

Thanksgiving for spiritual riches in Christ, Ephesians 1:3–14

For the Ephesian Christians, Ephesians 1:16–23; 3:14–19

For the Philippian Christians, Philippians 1:3–11

For the church at Colosse, Colossians 1:3–14

For the Thessalonian Christians,
1 Thessalonians 1:2–3; 2:13;
3:9–13; 5:23; 2 Thessalonians 1:3;
2:13, 16–17; 3:16

For Timothy, 2 Timothy 1:3–4

For Philemon, Philemon 4–6

## Doxologies, praise to God, and benedictions:

Romans 16:25–27; Ephesians 3:20–21; Philippians 4:20; 1 Thessalonians 3:11–13; Hebrews 13:20–21; 1 Peter 5:10–11; 2 Peter 3:28; Jude 24–25

# The miracles of Jesus

| | Matthew | Mark | Luke | John |
|---|---|---|---|---|
| **Healing** | | | | |
| Man with leprosy | 8:2–3 | 1:40–42 | 5:12–13 | |
| Centurion's servant | 8:5–13 | | 7:1–10 | |
| Peter's mother-in-law | 8:14–15 | 1:30–31 | 4:38–39 | |
| Two demon-possessed men | 8:28–34 | 5:1–15 | 8:27–35 | |
| Paralysed man | 9:2–7 | 2:3–12 | 5:18–25 | |
| Woman with a haemorrhage | 9:20–22 | 5:25–29 | 8:43–48 | |
| Two blind men | 9:27–31 | | | |
| Man mute and possessed | 9:32–33 | | | |
| Man with a shrivelled hand | 12:10–13 | 3:1–5 | 6:6–10 | |
| Man blind, mute and possessed | 12:22 | | 11:14 | |
| Canaanite woman's daughter | 15:21–28 | 7:24–30 | | |
| Boy with epilepsy | 17:14–18 | 9:17–29 | 9:38–43 | |
| Bartimaeus, and another blind man | 20:29–34 | 10:46–52 | 18:35–43 | |
| Deaf and mute man | | 7:31–37 | | |
| Man possessed, synagogue | | 1:23–36 | 4:33–35 | |
| Blind man at Bethsaida | | 8:22–26 | | |
| Crippled woman | | | 13:11–13 | |
| Man with dropsy | | | 14:1–4 | |
| Ten men with leprosy | | | 17:11–19 | |
| Malcus' ear | | | 22:50–51 | |
| Official's son at Capernaum | | | | 4:46–54 |
| Sick man, Pool of Bethesda | | | | 5:1–9 |
| Man born blind | | | | 9 |
| | | | | |
| **Command over the forces of nature** | | | | |
| Calming of the storm | 8:23–27 | 4:37–41 | 8:22–25 | |
| Walking on the water | 14:25 | 6:48–51 | | 6:19–21 |
| 5,000 people fed | 14:15–21 | 6:35–44 | 9:12–17 | 6:5–13 |
| 4,000 people fed | 15:32–38 | 8:1–9 | | |
| Coin in the fish's mouth | 17:24–27 | | | |
| Fig-tree withered | 21:18–22 | 11:12–14, 20–26 | | |
| Catch of fish | | | 5:1–11 | |
| Water turned into wine | | | | 2:1–11 |
| Another catch of fish | | | | 21:1–11 |
| | | | | |
| **Bringing the dead back to life** | | | | |
| Jairus' daughter | 9:18–19, 23–25 | 5:22–24, 38–42 | 8:41–42, 49–56 | |
| Widow of Nain's son | | | 7:11–15 | |
| Lazarus | | | | 11:1–44 |

# The parables of Jesus

| | Matthew | Mark | Luke |
|---|---|---|---|
| Lamp under a bowl | 5:14–15 | 4:21–22 | 8:16; 11:33 |
| Houses on rock and on sand | 7:24–27 | | 6:47–49 |
| New cloth on an old garment | 9:16 | 2:21 | 5:36 |
| New wine in old wineskins | 9:17 | 2:22 | 5:37–38 |
| Sower and soils | 13:3–8, 18–23 | 4:3–8, 13–20 | 8:5–8, 11–15 |
| Mustard seed | 13:31–32 | 4:30–32 | 13:18–19 |
| Weeds | 13:24–30 | | |
| Yeast | 13:33 | | 13:20–21 |
| Hidden treasure | 13:44 | | |
| Pearl of great value | 13:45–46 | | |
| Net | 13:47–48 | | |
| Lost sheep | 18:12–13 | | 15:4–6 |
| Unforgiving servant | 18:23–24 | | |
| Workers in the vineyard | 20:1–16 | | |
| Two sons | 21:28–31 | | |
| Tenants | 21:33–41 | 12:1–9 | 20:9–16 |
| Wedding feast | 22:2–14 | | |
| Lesson of the fig-tree | 24:32–33 | 13:28–29 | 21:29–32 |
| Ten young women | 25:1–13 | | |
| Three servants | 25:14–30 | | |
| Sheep and goats | 25:31–46 | | |
| Growing seed | | 4:26–29 | |
| Two debtors | | | 7:41–43 |
| Good Samaritan | | | 10:30–37 |
| Friend in need | | | 11:5–8 |
| Rich fool | | | 12:16–21 |
| Alert servants | | | 12:35–40 |
| Wise manager | | | 12:42–48 |
| Unfruitful fig-tree | | | 13:6–9 |
| Places of honour at the wedding-feast | | | 14:7–14 |
| Great banquet and the reluctant guests | | | 14:16–24 |
| Counting the cost | | | 14:28–33 |
| Lost coin | | | 15:8–10 |
| The prodigal son | | | 15:11–32 |
| Shrewd manager | | | 16:1–8 |
| Rich man and Lazarus | | | 16:19–31 |
| The master and his servant | | | 17:7–10 |
| The persistent widow and the corrupt judge | | | 18:2–5 |
| The Pharisee and the tax collector | | | 18:10–14 |
| Gold coins | | | 19:12–27 |

# Passages for use on special occasions and in times of need

## Special occasions

### Ascension Day
Psalms 24:7–10; 68; 18; 110; 1; Luke 24:36–53; John 14:1–21; 16:7; 17:5; Acts 1:1–14; 2:33–36; 3:20–21; 5:31; 7:56; Romans 8:31–34; Ephesians 1:20–23; 4:7–16; Philippians 2:9–11; Colossians 3:1–17; 1 Timothy 3:16; Hebrews 4:14–16; 7:24–25; 9:24; 10:12.

### Baptism; presentation of children; confirmation
Genesis 17; Leviticus 26:9–12; Joshua 1:5–9; 1 Samuel 1:27–28; Psalms 1; 23; 111; 115; 119:1–24; 121; Proverbs 8:32–36; Ecclesiastes 12:1; Isaiah 41:10; 43:1; Micah 6:8; Matthew 3:11–17; 10:32–33; 28:18–20; Mark 10:13–16; 16:16; John 3:1–21; 6:68; 8:12; 15:1–17; Acts 2; 8:36–40; 16:30–33; 19:1–6; 22:16; Romans 6:1–14; 10:9; 1 Corinthians 1:13–17; 7:14; 12:13; 15:1–10; 2 Corinthians 5:17; Galatians 3:26–28; Ephesians 3:14–21; 4:1–6; 5:25–27; Philippians 1:1–11; 2:12–13; 4:4–9; Colossians

2:6–14; 1 Timothy 6:11–16; Titus 3:4–7; Hebrews 13:20–21; 1 Peter 3:18–22; 2 Peter 3:18; Jude 24; Revelation 3:11.

### Bereavement
See pages 175–76.

### Birthday
Deuteronomy 32:1–12; Joshua 1:1–9; 1 Samuel 7:12–13; 2 Samuel 7:18–29; Psalms 1; 23; 25; 32; 34; 37:3–7; 39:1–6; 90; 91; 103; 116; 121; 126; 127; 136; 139; 145; Proverbs 3:5–8; Isaiah 12; 26:3–4; 41:10; 43:1–3; 46:4; Jeremiah 6:16; Lamentations 3:22–26; Matthew 6:33–34; 10:29–31; Luke 1:46–55; John 6:35; 8:12; 10:1–30; Acts 14:15–17; Romans 8:28–39; 11:33–36; 1 Corinthians 1:3–9; 2 Corinthians 12:9–10; Ephesians 1:3–14; Philippians 3:4–14; 4:4–7; Hebrews 10:23; James 3:13–18; 4:13–17; 1 John 1:7–9; 3:1–3.

### Christmas and New Year
Suggested reading plan
December 16: Isaiah 7:10–17

*The sign of Immanuel*
December 17: Isaiah 9:1–7
*To us a child is born*
December 18: Micah 5:1–5
*A promised ruler from Bethlehem*
December 19: Luke 1:5–25
*Preparing for the Lord*
December 20: Luke 1:26–38
*Jesus' birth foretold*
December 21: Luke 1:39–56
*Mary and Elizabeth*
December 22: Luke 1:67–80
*Zechariah's song*
December 23: Colossians 1:15–20
*Who Jesus is*
December 24: John 1:1–18
*The Word became flesh*
December 25: Luke 2:1–7
*The Saviour is born*
December 26: Luke 2:8–20
*The shepherds and the angels*
December 27: Matthew 2:1–12
*The Magi worship Jesus*
December 28: Luke 2:21–32
*Jesus is presented in the temple*
December 29: Luke 2:36–38
*The redemption of Jerusalem*
December 30: Matthew 2:13–18
*Jesus is kept safe*
December 31: Psalm 90
*Teach us to number our days*
January 1: Exodus 33:7–23
*'Show me your glory'*
January 2: Philippians 3:4–14
*Pressing on to the goal*
January 3: Joshua 1:1–9
*Be strong and courageous*

January 4: Matthew 6:25–34
*Do not worry*
January 5: Romans 8:28–39
*More than conquerors*
January 6: Philippians 4:4–9
*Rejoice in the Lord*

## Easter

Suggested reading plan
Palm Sunday: Luke 19:28–44
*The approach to Jerusalem*
Monday: Luke 19:45–48
*Jesus at the temple*
Tuesday: Philippians 2:5–11
*Obedient to death*
Wednesday: 1 Peter 2:21–25
*Christ suffered for you*
Maundy Thursday: Luke 22:7–71;
John 17 *The last supper; Jesus' prayer*
Good Friday: Luke 23; Isaiah 53
*The crucifixion*
Saturday: Matthew 27:62–66
*The guard at the tomb*
Easter Day: Matthew 28:1–20
*The resurrection*
Easter Monday: John 20:24–31
*My Lord and my God!*
Tuesday: 1 Corinthians 15:12–58
*Victory over death*
Wednesday: Acts 2:22–41
*Why Jesus died*
Thursday: Romans 1:1–17
*Jesus Christ our Lord*
Friday: Romans 6:5–14
*United with him*
Saturday: Colossians 3:1–4
*Raised with Christ*

# 'You can rest for a while'

Jesus told his apostles, 'Let us go off by ourselves to some place where we will be alone and you can rest for a while.' (Mark 6:31, GNB). Here are two weeks' holiday readings of Jesus' parables as recorded in Luke's Gospel. These readings could be used on holiday to quietly think about our priorities concerning Christ's kingdom and our following him in our daily lives.

| Day 1 | Luke 8:5–15 | The sower and the soils |
| Day 2 | Luke 10:25–37 | The good Samaritan |
| Day 3 | Luke 12:13–21 | The rich fool |
| Day 4 | Luke 12:35–48 | Be alert! |
| Day 5 | Luke 13:20–21 | Parables of the kingdom |
| Day 6 | Luke 14:7–14 | True humility |
| Day 7 | Luke 14:15–23 | The great banquet |
| Day 8 | Luke 14:25–35 | Counting the cost |
| Day 9 | Luke 15:11–32 | The two sons |
| Day 10 | Luke 16:1–15 | The shrewd manager |
| Day 11 | Luke 17:7–10 | The master and his servant |
| Day 12 | Luke 18:1–8 | The persistent widow |
| Day 13 | Luke 18:9–14 | The Pharisee and the tax collector |
| Day 14 | Luke 19:11–27 | Faithfulness |

Sunday: Revelation 1:4–18
Alive for ever and ever

## Pentecost (Whitsun)
Leviticus 23:15–22; Deuteronomy 16:9–12; Isaiah 32:15; 44:2–3; Jeremiah 31:31–34; Ezekiel 36:22–28; 37:1–14; Joel 2:28–32; Matthew 3:11–17; John 3:1–8; 7:37–39; 14; 15–26; 15:26; 16:7–15; Acts 1:8; 2; 4:31; 6:5; 10; 19:1–7; Romans 5:5; 8:1–16, 26–27; 1 Corinthians 2:12–14; 12–14; 2 Corinthians 3:17–18; Galatians 4:6; 5:22–23; Ephesians 4:30; 5:18; 1 Thessalonians 5:19.

## Thanksgiving
Deuteronomy 6:10–19; 8; Psalms 23; 33; 65; 67; 95; 100; 103; 104; 107; 111; 126; 136; 145; 147; Isaiah 12; Jeremiah 5:20–24; Luke 12:13–34; John 6:26–40; Acts 14:17; 1 Corinthians 3:5–9; Hebrews 13:15–16; Revelation 5.

## Wedding day

Genesis 2:18–25; Joshua 24:15; Ruth 1:16–17; Psalms 37:3–7; 67; 84; 100; 103; 118:24–29; 121; 127; 128; 139; Proverbs 31:10–31; Matthew 19:3–9; John 2:1–11; 1 Corinthians 7; 13; Ephesians 5:22–23; Colossians 3:12–4:1; Hebrews 13:4; 1 Peter 3:1–7.

# In times of need

The bible contains many promises of comfort that can help and encourage us in times of sorrow, difficulty or stress. Here are some passages that show us God's help at different times in our lives. You could read and think about these when:

## • You feel afraid

'I prayed to the LORD, and he answered me; he freed me from all my fears.' (Psalm 34:4, GNB).
See also Psalms 27; 46; 56; 91; Matthew 8:23–27.

## • You are anxious or worried

'Leave all your worries with him, because he cares for you.' (1 Peter 5:7, GNB).
See also Isaiah 43:1–13; Matthew 6:25–34; 11:28; Philippians 4:4–7.

## • You have been bereaved

'Happy are those who mourn; God will comfort them!' (Matthew 5:4, GNB).

See also Psalm 23; John 11:21–27; 1 Corinthians 15:51–57; 1 Thessalonians 4:13–18; Revelation 21:1–5.

## • You feel discouraged

'Why am I so sad? Why am I so troubled? I will put my hope in God, and once again I will praise him, my saviour and my God.' (Psalm 42:5, GNB).
See also Psalms 34:18; 40:1–3; Lamentations 3:20–23; Romans 8:28–39; 2 Corinthians 4:7–18.

## • You have doubts

'The father at once cried out, "I do have faith, but not enough. Help me to have more!" ' (Mark 9:24, GNB).
See also Isaiah 40:27–28; Matthew 11:1–6; John 20:19–29; Acts 17:22–28.

## • You feel you have done wrong

'But God has shown us how much he loves us – it was while we were still sinners that Christ died for us!' (Romans 5:8, GNB).
See also Psalm 51; Luke 15:11–24.

## • You feel far from God

'What my Father has given me is greater than everything, and no one can snatch them away from the Father's care.' (John 10:29, GNB).

See also Psalm 139:1–18; Acts 17:24–31; James 4:8.

## • You are ill or in pain

'My grace is all you need, for my power is greatest when you are weak.' (2 Corinthians 12:9, GNB).
See also Psalm 103:1–4; Romans 8:18–25; 2 Corinthians 4:16–18.

## • You feel lonely

'Do not be afraid – I am with you! I am your God – let nothing terrify you!' (Isaiah 41:10, GNB).
See also Psalms 23; 73:23–24; Isaiah 49:14–16; John 14:15–21.

## • You need peace

'You, LORD, give perfect peace to those who keep their purpose firm and put their trust in you.' (Isaiah 26:3, GNB).
See also John 14:27; Romans 5:1–5; Philippians 4:4–7.

## • You are tempted

'Our High Priest is not one who cannot feel sympathy for our weaknesses. On the contrary, we have a High Priest who was tempted in every way that we are, but did not sin.' (Hebrews 4:15,GNB).
See also Luke 4:1–13; Ephesians 6:10–20; James 1:12–18; 1 Peter 5:8–9.

## • You are tired or weak

'Come to me, all of you who are tired from carrying heavy loads, and I will give you rest. Take my yoke and put it on you, and learn from me, because I am gentle and humble in spirit; and you will find rest. For the yoke I will give you is easy, and the load I will put on you is light.' (Matthew 11:28–30, GNB).
See also Joshua 1:6–9; Isaiah 40:28–31; 2 Corinthians 4:16–18; 12:9–10; Philippians 4:12–13.

# Where to find help in the book of Psalms

## When you feel ...

Afraid, 3; 4; 27; 46; 49; 56; 91; 118
Alone, 9; 10; 12; 13; 27; 40; 43
'Burned out', 6; 63
Cheated, 41
Confused, 10; 12; 73
Depressed, 27; 34; 42; 43; 88; 143
Distressed, 13; 25; 31; 40; 107
Elated, 19; 96
Guilty, 19; 32; 38; 51
Hateful, 11
Impatient, 13; 27; 37; 40
Insecure, 3; 5; 12; 91
Insulted, 41; 70
Jealous, 37
Like quitting, 29; 43; 145
Lost, 23; 139
Overwhelmed, 25; 69; 142
Penitent/sorry, 37; 51; 66

## When you're facing …

## When you want …

# Bibliography

## Section 1

David and Pat Alexander (Eds), *The Lion Handbook to the Bible,* Lion.

J. D. Douglas, Merrill C. Tenney (Eds), *The New International Dictionary of the Bible,* Zondervan/ Marshall Pickering.

Alan S. Duthie, *Bible Translations and how to choose between them,* Paternoster.

William Hendriksen, *Survey of the Bible,* Baker.

Andrew E. Hill, *Baker's Handbook of Bible Lists,* Baker

*Illustrated Bible Dictionary,* Inter-Varsity/Tyndale House.

Peter Jeffery, *Christian Handbook,* Evangelical Press of Wales

Eugene A. Nida, *Good News For Everyone: How to Use the Good News Bible,* Word.

Hy. Pickering, *1000 Wonderful Things about the Bible,* Pickering & Inglis.

Phyllis Thompson, *Matched With His Hour,* Word.

E. E. Wallis & M. A. Bennett, *Two thousand Tongues to go,* Hodder & Stoughton/Harper & Row.

## Section 2

John J. Davis, *Biblical Numerology,* Baker.

W. B. Fulghum, Jr, *Dictionary of Biblical Allusions in English Literature,* Holt, Rinehart & Winston.

David Lyle Jeffrey (Ed), *A Dictionary of Biblical Tradition in English Literature,* Eerdmans.

Martin H. Manser (Comp.), *Chambers Bible Quotations,* Chambers.

## Section 3

Robert Atwan & Laurance Wieder (Eds), *Chapters into Verse,* Oxford University Press (2 volumes).

J.C.J. Metford, *Dictionary of Christian Lore and Legend,* Thames and Hudson Ltd, London.

Bruce M. Metzger & Michael D. Coogan (Eds), *The Oxford Companion to the Bible,* Oxford University Press.

Keith White, *The Art of Faith,* Hunt & Thorpe.

## Section 4

J. Stephen Lang, *The Complete Book of Bible Trivia*, Tyndale House.

J.L. Meredith, *Meredith's Book of Bible Lists*, Bethany House.

Mark D. Taylor, *The Complete Book of Bible Literacy*, Tyndale House.

## Section 5

Brian M. Abshire, *Get more from your Bible: practical help from Bible study*, Scripture Union.

J.D.C. Anderson (Ed), *The Quiet Time*, Inter-Varsity.

Edward P. Clowney, *Christian Meditation*, Craig Press.

Gordon D. Fee, Douglas Stuart, *How to Read the Bible for all its worth*, Zondervan/Scripture Union.

*Good News Study Bible*, Bible Societies/HarperCollins.

Joyce Huggett, *Listening to God*, Hodder & Stoughton.

Martin H. Manser (Comp), *Concise Book of Bible Quotations*, Lion.

John Sherrill, *My Friend, the Bible*, Chosen Books.

Alan M. Stibbs (Ed), *Search the Scriptures*, Inter-Varsity.

Geoffrey Thomas, *Reading the Bible*, Banner of Truth.

David L. Thompson, *Bible study that works*, Zondervan/Scripture Union.

John White and others, *Hear the Word*, Inter-Varsity.

# Acknowledgements

Martin H. Manser wishes to acknowledge the help of many individuals and organizations in the writing of this book, including Rosalind Desmond (particularly for the compilation of additional material on the new edition), Christine Smith, James Catford, Geoffrey Hunt, Alison Watkins, John Hanson, Kathleen Webb, and Olive Page; the Buckinghamshire Country Reference Library, University of London Library, Bible Society, American Bible Society, International Bible Society, Wycliffe Bible Translators, Zondervan Bible Publishers, Hodder & Stoughton, The Gideons International, Theodore Roosevelt Birthplate NHS.

**Section 1** 'Bible overview' from *The Student Bible*, Zondervan/Hodder & Stoughton; 'The Bible in English', 'The book of books', 'Chapters and verses' from *The New International Dictionary of the Bible*, Ed. J.D. Douglas and M.C. Tenney, Zondervan/Marshall Pickering; 'The morning star of the Reformation' from *Christian Handbook*, Peter Jeffery, Evangelical Press of Wales; 'Out of the mouths of babes ...' from *Christian Bookseller Review*, July 1989; 'A very important city' from *A Bible for Today & Tomorrow: The Story of the English Bible and the New International Version*, Hodder & Stoughton.

**Section 2** Material adapted from *Chambers Bible Quotations*, comp. Martin H. Manser, Chambers and *Dictionary of Eponyms*, Martin H. Manser, Sphere; 'Christian names' from *Guinness Book of Names*, Leslie Dunkling, Guinness; 'The Dominion of Canada' adapted from the *Canadian Encyclopedia*; '70 – an administrative number' adapted from *The Illustrated Bible Dictionary*, Inter-Varsity Press/Tyndale House; '153 – a wonderful number' from *Biblical Numerology*, John J. Davis, Baker; extracts in '666 – the number of the beast' from *The Message of Revelation: I saw heaven opened*, Michael Wilcock, Inter-Varsity Press and *More than Conquerors*, William Hendriksen, Baker.

**Section 3** *My Bible and I* by Charles Sandford quoted in Sunshine and

Shadow, Back to Bible Broadcast, 1962, from *212 Victory Poems*, Zondervan Publishing House; panel on 'Money' adapted from Martin H. Manser and Martin J. Selman, *Macmillan Bible Dictionary*, (Macmillan 1998); *Revelation*, F.H.Wrintmore, quoted with permission of the London City Mission; 'Bill's Bible' from *Renewal*, August 1988; 'Stanley's last book' and 'Comfort in death' from *1200 Notes, Quotes, and Anecdotes*, A. Naismith, Pickering and Inglis; 'God still speaks' from *The Fight*, John White, Inter-Varsity Press; 'Royal standards' from *Truth for Life: A Personal Exposition of the Epistle of James*, John Blanchard, H.E. Walter/Evangelical Press; 'The power of God's word' from *1000 Wonderful Things about the Bible*, Hy. Pickering, Pickering & Inglis; 'In solitary confinement … but not alone', from *Fear No Evil: A personal struggle with cancer*, David C.K. Watson, Hodder & Stoughton; 'The experience of Bible translation from *The Story of the New International Version*, New York International Bible Society; 'Lord Shaftesbury, social reformer' from *The Life and Work of*

*the 7th Earl of Shaftesbury*, E. Hodder, Cassell; 'William Wilberforce, the liberator' from *Sketches from Church History*, S.M. Houghton, Banner of Truth and *Wilberforce*, R. Coupland, Collins; 'Thoroughly equipped' from *Quotable Quotations*, Lloyd Cory, Victor Books, Scripture Press; quotation in 'God spoke to them through Romans' from *Sketches from Church History*, S.M. Houghton.

**Section 5** 3-Track plan for reading the Bible and 'Where to find …' from *The Student Bible*; 'Miracles of Jesus', 'Parables of Jesus', 'Prayers of the Bible' from *The Lion Concise Book of Bible Quotations*, comp. Martin H. Manser, Lion; 'In times of need' adapted from *Bible Promises: Outlines for Christian Living*, Martin H. Manser, Marshall Pickering/Zondervan; 'Where to find help in the book of Psalms' from *Life Application Bible* © 1988 by Tyndale House Publishers, Inc., Wheaton, IL 60189. *Life Application* is a trademark of Tyndale House Publishers, Inc. Used by permission. All rights reserved.

# Biblical Index

| | | | | | |
|---|---|---|---|---|---|
| 28:17 | 92 | 11:31–33 | 141 | **Joshua** | |
| 28:18 | 92 | 11:31–34 | 94 | overview of, | 7 |
| 28:19 | 92 | 13–14 | 139 | 1:1 | 143 |
| 30:23 | 92 | 13:16 | 138 | 2 | 79 |
| 30:24 | 92 | 15:23 | 96 | 2:4 | 142 |
| 30:34 | 92 | 17:1–9 | 142 | 4:18 | 31 |
| 33:11 | 31, 146 | 17:1–13 | 64 | 6 | 79 |
| 35:30–31 | 140 | 21:4–9 | 141 | 6:4 | 116 |
| 39:10 | 92 | 22:21–41 | 141 | 9:1 | 144 |
| 39:12 | 92 | 23:23 | 38 | 9:21 | 57 |
| 39:13 | 92 | 26:5 | 121 | 10:13 | 145 |
| | | 30:2 | 31 | 14–15 | 139 |
| **Leviticus** | | 31:51 | 31 | 23:14 | 58 |
| overview of, | 7 | 33:38–39 | 144 | 24:2 | 65 |
| 2:1 | 142 | 35:20 | 31 | | |
| 2:4 | 142 | | | **Judges** | |
| 2:13–14 | 142 | **Deuteronomy** | | overview of, | 7 |
| 5:11 | 142 | overview of, | 7 | 3:9 | 138 |
| 6:22 | 121 | 5:1–21 | 144 | 3:10 | 65 |
| 11:1–8 | 141 | 5:26 | 65 | 6–7 | 70 |
| 13:29–37 | 143 | 6:4 | 80 | 6:24 | 65 |
| 16:20–22 | 120 | 8:3 | 145 | 12:4–6 | 46 |
| 16:29–30 | 81 | 12:15 | 94 | 13 | 143 |
| 19:10 | 94 | 14:3–8 | 141 | 13:15 | 94 |
| 19:18 | 145 | 14:5 | 94 | 16:4 | 144 |
| 23:5 | 93 | 14:26 | 94 | 16:4–22 | 68 |
| 23:6 | 93 | 16:9 | 93 | 17:4 | 91 |
| 23:23 | 93 | 18:15 | 145 | 20:1 | 78 |
| 23:26 | 93 | 21:23 | 145 | 21:25 | 143 |
| 23:33 | 93 | 27:2–3 | 117 | | |
| 26:12 | 145 | 29:6 | 94 | **Ruth** | |
| | | 32:2 | 106 | overview of, | 7 |
| **Numbers** | | 32:10 | 47 | 1:1 | 143 |
| overview of, | 7 | 34:10 | 120 | 1:16 | 139 |
| 6:24–26 | 139 | 34:12 | 143 | 1:20 | 138 |
| 11:5 | 92, 94 | | | 1:22 | 138 |
| 11:16 | 81 | | | 2:23 | 94 |

| | |
|---|---|
| 3:15 | 34 |
| 4:22 | 143 |
| **1 Samuel** | |
| overview of, | 8 |
| 1–2 | 138 |
| 1:11 | 65 |
| 3:1–21 | 139 |
| 3:10 | 139 |
| 5:6 | 97 |
| 6:7 | 141 |
| 9–10 | 138 |
| 10:9–11 | 140 |
| 10:11 | 140 |
| 13:4 | 31 |
| 13:14 | 47 |
| 14:49 | 139 |
| 16:7 | 144 |
| 17:34–35 | 141 |
| 17 | 68 |
| 17:7 | 94 |
| 17:38 | 95 |
| 17:40 | 95 |
| 17:45 | 95 |
| 17:49 | 121 |
| 18:27 | 139 |
| 20 | 68 |
| 22:1–2 | 77 |
| 25 | 64 |
| 25:3–42 | 138 |
| 26:21 | 57 |
| 28:24 | 31 |
| 31:4 | 140 |
| 31:8 | 144 |

# Subject Index